DESIGN

MARC WALTER

RESEARCH

CATHERINE DONZEL

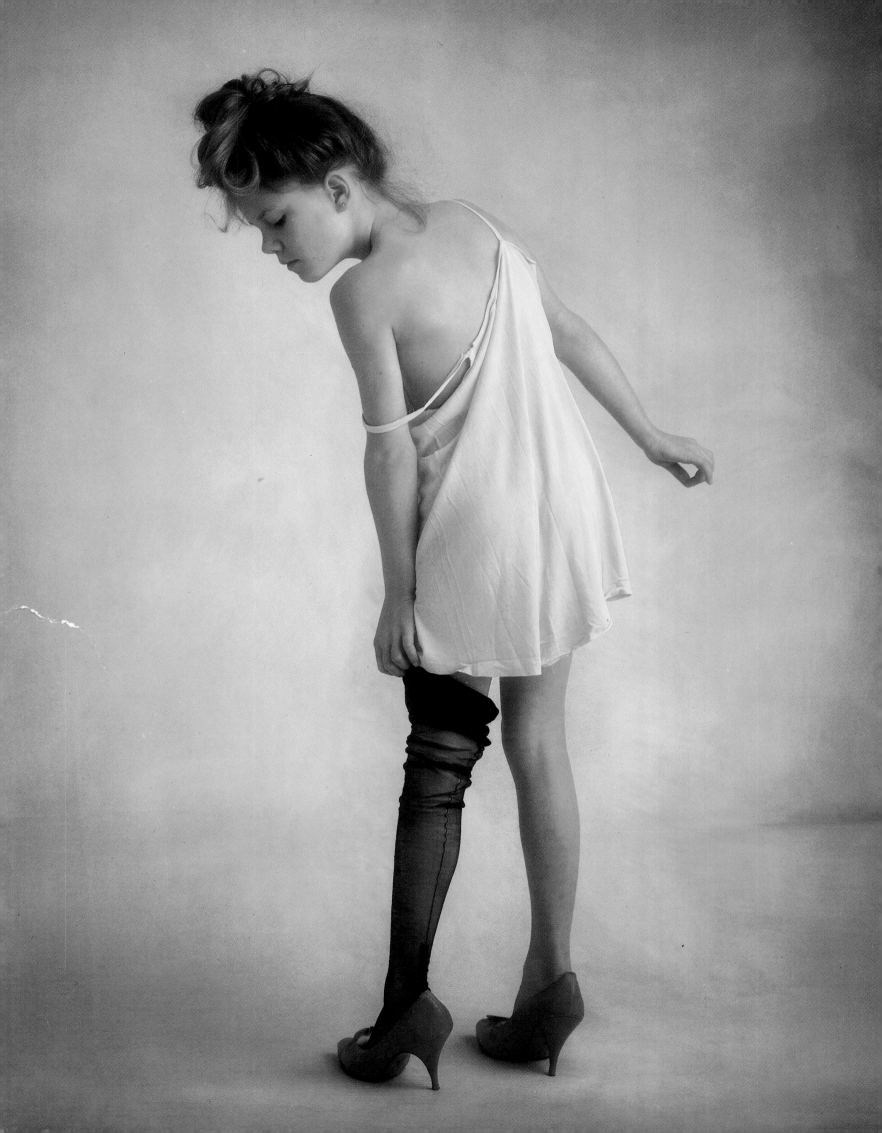

CECIL SAINT–LAURENT

THE GREAT BOOK
OF
LINGERIE

THE VENDOME PRESS

The Vendome Press
515 Madison Avenue
New York, N.Y. 10022

Distributed in the United States by
Rizzoli International Publications
597 Fifth Avenue
New York, N.Y. 10017

Distributed in Canada by Methuen Publications

© Text, Cécil Saint-Laurent
© Times Editions
422 Thomson Road, Singapore. 1129
First published in this edition
in 1986

Printed by Tien Wah Press, Singapore

Library of Congress Cataloguing-in-Publication Data
Saint-Laurent, Cécil, 1919 –
The Great book of lingerie.
1. Lingerie   1. Title
TT670. S25 1986   391'.42
ISBN 0-86565-072-1

Preceding pages: Page 1: Underwear boutique, Lisbon.
Photo by F.X. Bouchart.
Pages 2-3: Photo Valérie Winckler
Page 4: Photo François Gillet
Pages 6-7: Sales campaign for the French brand Rosy, in
the 80s. Photo by Steve Hiett.

C O N T E N T S

*P*hilosophers often contrast appearance and reality. Clothing unites these opposites and reveals hidden secrets.

Appearances clearly conceal mysteries only hinted at — the gentle swellings of men beneath the waistline or women's blouses filled out by breasts; two images that clearly differentiate the sexes. Clothing is designed to accentuate this contrast and to reveal that which is only barely suggested. This is indispensable if the games between male and female are to be successful.

One can imagine a country where clothing would no longer distinguish between men and women. Quite recently, both in Europe and in the States, fevered brains conceived — and pleaded for — the idea of unisex clothing. Then this idea contaminated the minds of some distinguished persons and within a few months one of my own friends made the following remarks that were quite revealing. First he announced "The era of the dress is now over". He was undoubtedly influenced by his girlfriend who slavishly followed the fluctuations of fashion and did not adhere to her own fashion philosophy; in other words, to a philosophy of change applying an inner vision to the limitations of shape available.

A few years later, the same man, being absolutely indifferent to an overwhelming comeback of skirts and dresses, noticed a bicycle with a curved crossbar anchored to a lamp post on Boulevard Saint Germain and said; "I don't understand why bicycle makers are still producing those bicycles with that space for dresses, since they do not exist anymore!" As he spoke, a young girl appeared in a flowered dress, untied her vehicle and cycled away. He did not look at her, preferring his own theories to the reality of the situation.

A little later, almost at the same place, I told him that as I was walking down Rue du Dragon, I saw a young woman getting out of a car and I could tell from the way she moved that she was not wearing any panties. He listened to me, nodded and said, "Not wearing panties is only interesting under slacks". Clothing is undoubtedly an area in which intelligence is most often at odds with prejudice and habit!

Fashion designers often ignore the sexual implications of clothes; they see themselves as architects, and design dresses as if they were designing a building. Even Stéphane Mallarmé, when he ran a magazine called "La Dernière Mode" (The Latest Fashion) resorted to feminine pseudonyms such as Miss Satin, Marguerite de Ponty, Zigy, Olympia. His sensitivity was expressed by a melange of colours, fabrics and words. Covered with jet beads and wrapped in gauze, feathers and tulle, the woman dressed by Mallarmé is a cold and impenetrable abstraction; she has fake flowers in her hair made by Louise and Lucie who "have the fingers of morning roses, but an artificial morning, with calyx and pistil made of fabric that open out." The woman has no fragrance

*N*asstasja Kinski, picture from the movie *Maria's Lovers*, 1983. Left: "The history of feminine underwear revives all those foolish flights of imagination." Photo by Robert Doisneau.

herself but wears scents called "Crème-neige", "Lait d'hébé", "Opoponax", "Liang-Chang", "Nord Celtique", the perfume as evocative and lovely as the words themselves.

At the time when undergarments were considered as additional protective clothing, the sensuous relationship between women and clothes was more threatened than by unisex trends. The multiple layers of imprisoning undergarments protecting the woman from undesirable glances and hindering free movement, were worse than simple panties worn under a pair of jeans. Women used to be confined in a corset from the shoulders down to the thighs and this corset was worn over an undershirt. In addition to that they wore long baggy drawers and a corset-cover down to the waistline where petticoats were gathered. The dress was a sheath that concealed the shape of the body, limited the number of undergarments and restricted their shape to the very simple.

Mallarmé amused himself by re-employing the many words used late in the last century to describe their clothes: insertion, braid, trimming, applique, crepe, tassel, gathers, blouse, corselet, burnouse, basque, cape, train, tail, flounce, sheath, ruche, breastplate, pouffe, guipure, panel, scarf, shawl, muff. He described the precious fabrics much sought after by the rich using a veritable torrent of words. The list is almost endless so I will give only a sample: brocaded, embossed, quilted, woollen cloth and wool-blend cloth, suede and satin, crêpe de Chine or Islam crêpe, tulle, serge, muslin, jacona, lawn, rep, Scottish wool, cheviotte, flannel, silk, velvet, silk chiffon, moire, organdy, gauze, trimmed with laces, gold and silver embroideries, silk embroideries, feathers and furs. There is one word, the meaning of which is very clear: "sexy". Women were said to be "sexy" in the reign of Louis-Philippe and again during the First World War when short tunics and panty combinations came into vogue.

The history of underwear is not very well documented. It has no place in historical novels, it is scorned by historians who, even though they sometimes refer to it, skim over it making many mistakes in the process. Here is one example. In the book on the escape of Louis XVI to Varennes, Paul and Pierrette Girault de Coursac criticized Choiseul, a chronicler who insisted that he had provided the king with an escape plan.

The authors wrote: "Out of seven people riding horses, or rather trying to ride horses, six were women in women's clothes, consisting of the traditional dress which at that time was a long narrow sheath; women's undergarments consisted of an undershirt, stockings, a petticoat and sometimes a corset. Panties and drawers did not appear before the 19th century. As it is impossible to ride sidesaddle on a Hussar saddle (French-style saddle), all six women would have had to ride astride. Therefore they would have had to tuck their

"As they were about to get engaged, Catherine became worried by the strange behaviour of her husband ..." Marcello Mastroianni. Left: Saucy postcard, France, 20s.

dresses up to the waist and ride bare-thighed, six leagues on a very bad track all the way to the town of Dun. Can you imagine! Perhaps the Hussars should have lent their trousers with the horses!"

Both historians agreed that the mistake was due to the fact that the Memoirs they referred to were published in 1822 and that in those days "women wore flounced drawers longer than the skirt and that everybody, including Choiseul, forgot how people dressed in 1791."

In fact in 1822 women did not wear flounced drawers under their skirts. Those historians knew how undergarments looked in the Old Regime and wrongly supposed that after the Revolution and the Empire, they had drastically changed. In 1822, there were some underpants used exclusively for riding horses but they were not particularly fashionable or popular. The chronicler accused by Paul et Pierrette Girault de Coursac could not be influenced by a new trend, since there was no new trend. Still what he said is true and proof that the knowledge of women's underwear can be related to the interpretation of a famous historic incident.

I wrote this book because since my teenage years I have been fascinated by items of clothing that were deemed worthy of worship; panties and even corsets trigger off a kind of mystical ecstasy that somehow unites men with the feminine world. Here, contemplation is synonymous with action and in the fantasy a simple look becomes a gesture. The history of women's undergarments revives all men's foolish flights of imagination. While men's undergarments are very rational, without emotional connotations, women's undergarments have a sensual meaning.

During Antiquity, Greek women used to be wrapped in a bandage at the waist under their dresses which was absolutely useless; its only purpose was to enhance the feminine curves of the body. Similarly Roman women used to wear garters above the knee which held up nothing, since tights did not exist then: they were designed to stimulate a subtle desire in men — a desire that was close to fetishism.

Fetishism means the confusion of the part with the whole and is proof that a small specific detail concentrates sensuousness and intensifies it. That is why Roman women created and adopted more than half a dozen undergarments, lauded with great emotion by dissolute poets.

Couples that these days applaud a show at the Crazy Horse are very aware of its beauty and its perfection, and watching those enchanting dancers wearing garterbelts they become part of a mystery, transported into one of those dreamlike ceremonies that date back to mythology. All they want to do is to continue the romance and the erotic ceremony they have seen in the privacy of their own home.

Irving Klaw posing between two of his models. U.S.A., the 40s. In 1948, Irving Klaw became one of the (unknown) experts of "sado-masochism and bondage photography". Thousands of pictures were taken to illustrate the various possibilities of sado-erotic underwear. In 1963, he was sentenced for having used the U.S. mail to send obscene pictures and was forced to destroy all the negatives. Indeed censorship has sometimes hindered the development of photography of feminine underwear. That is the reason why there are so few pictures or drawings in women's magazines of the "panties" (pantaloons) worn from the 19th century until the 1920s.
Left, above: *Reclining nude* – Egon Schiele, 1918; below: *Walli Wearing a Red Blouse.* Egon Shiele, 1913.

15

Over a thousand years the epic of women's undergarments was in fact an irresistible fantasy for both sexes: a fantasy that would be dazzling, covert, hypocritical or provocative. Before it is accepted, a new undergarment has to have some justification, but the male or female designers, those who wear them or those who just look at them, are quite aware that they do not quite fit into the world of reality and are simply a part of a reverie, a fantasy.

An undergarment has even more power and more meaning when it isn't there. From the 12th to 19th century, men have had only one thing on their minds — the essential biological difference that clearly distinguishes men from women. While men were enclosed in a confined system of clothing, women were exposed and naked, prey to a gust of wind, a glance, a fall, a false move or some intentional carelessness. As the most intimate area of the body remained uncovered and at the mercy of any assailant, it triggered off an emotional feeling that has not dimmed over the centuries. In the 17th century, the revealing fall of a court lady from her horse had great impact and was painted over and over again. In the 18th century, Fragonard painted a girl on a swing, focusing his attention on a boy glancing between the thighs of a young girl wearing wide petticoats. We know what he could see ...

In the 19th century, Winterhalter painted a young girl crossing a stream which showed the reflection of that secret place between her thighs. A few years later women adopted linen drawers that enclosed their body from the waist to the ankles. They were called "modesty tubes", which was very discouraging! But soon afterwards undergarments became more revealing. Drawers were slit between the thighs, they were more close fitting and worn with sexy stockings and garters. That was when a dance called "French Cancan" became very famous all over the world.

As long as men and women are mutually attracted, women will always be aware of the importance of undergarments. And they will always know that the game between the sexes is very complex and that nudity is an indispensable part of it. It is interesting to note that Manet, in his painting called "le dejeuner sur l'herbe" (The Picnic Lunch), painted a naked model sitting with guests in very formal dress. I wonder whether in the years to come women will take advantage of nudity? Nudity by the water, nudity under the dress. It is possible, but only hypothetical, for when it comes to the history of clothes, nothing is certain. Nevertheless the following pages show that I have managed to establish a few rules that have marked the changes in clothing. Those rules apply on a short-term basis but they may not apply in the longer future. Robida foresaw the helicopter and Jules Verne the submarine, but neither one could have foreseen the mini-skirt or the G-string.

In any case women's garments and in particular, the vocabulary used to

The Invisible Woman Henri Cadiou, 1966.
Left, above: Ileana II, John Kacere, 1982;
below: Greta, John Kacere, 1982.

describe them is a good way to expose the moral climate of various periods. In the 17th century women liked wearing very full dresses. It was a fantasy that dated back to the time of the Cretans, but it disappeared only to return later on. That is why women in the reign of Louis XIV wore three petticoats under their dresses, one was called "the modest", the middle one was called "the mischievous" and the last one, "the secret". Such words reflect the moral climate. Consequently the next corset that appeared was called "hussy". In the 18th century, the pouffe worn under the petticoat was called the *cul* (which translates in English as bum).

In contrast, the 19th century was influenced by Victorian codes of decency and women were then considered ethereal beings; saucy expressions were prohibited and the only way to avoid them was to use euphemisms. For instance names of colours were prettified — "moonlight grey", "Russian grey", "opal blue", "forget-me-not", "peacock", "twilight", "Havana", and later "pigeon throat" and "nymph's thigh".

In our day the secret word is "practical". As chroniclers try to document changes in clothing, they explain the shapes and curves without understanding them fully — missing all the warm, erotic fantasy they represent.

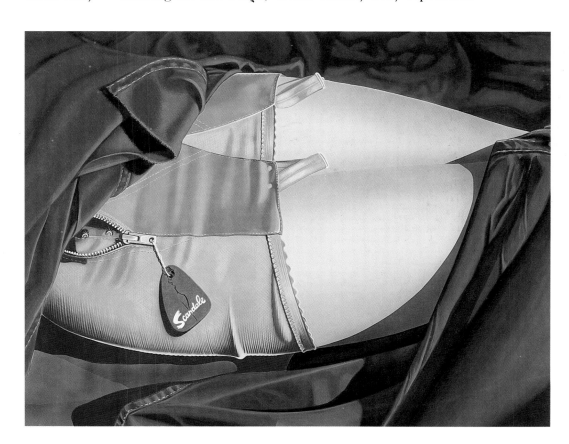

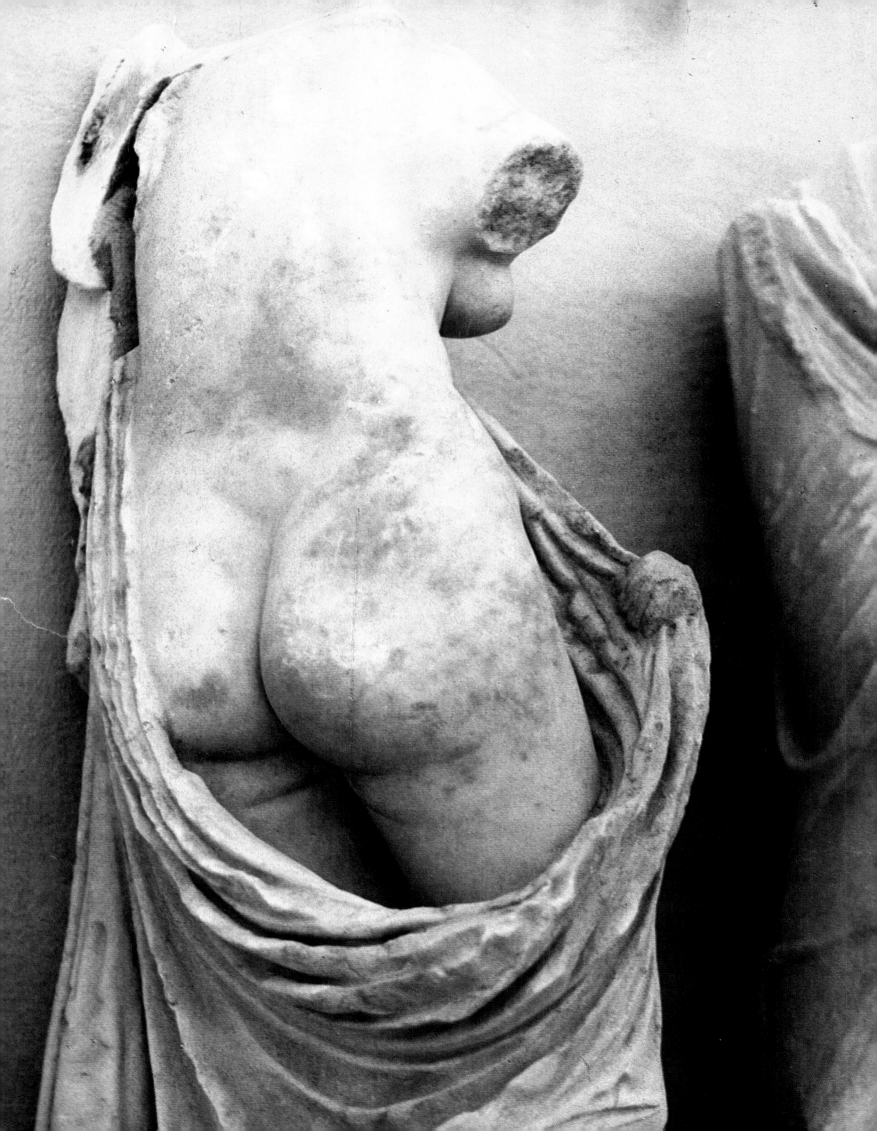

THE ORIGINS OF CLOTHING

If man wears clothes he does so of his own free will. It is a very natural mistake to think that clothing is of the same order as housing, farming or cattle-breeding, but whereas nature forces man to sleep, drink and eat, it does not force him to wear clothes except in extreme climates.

The Mediterranean peoples would still be as naked as the Amazonian Indians if they had only been aware of physiological needs. But the imagined requirements of the soul worried them just as much as those of the body, and so clothing was born.

Useless but neccessary, superfluous but fascinating, its very emergence proved man knew he was not an animal. The birth of clothing must be placed between that of religion and art, it cannot be compared with weapons, hunting implements or agricultural tools.

Clothing in this sense means anything that could adorn the human body, even a mere streak of paint. For clothing was first of all an ornament. Man drew stripes on the sides of pots, and also on his skin; the inclination to draw on stone walls made him draw on his own flesh, and eventually he came to consider these

Young girl dressing. Athenian bowl from Chiusi. Beginning of 5th century BC.
Left: Léto, Museum of Delos.

A Lady dressing, Djeserkaraseneb tomb, Thebes 1422-1411 BC. Slaves used to wear a very small embroidered G-string that free Egyptians would never dream of wearing, even under their tunics.

pastimes to be as basic and essential as the activities necessary to survival. The human skin is as smooth as the surface of carved stone; its uniform colour is ideal for painting.

The structure of the body includes slender parts which can be girded, curves from which things can be hung, protuberances which can be crowned, tapering shapes on which to fit circles until the volume keeps them in place. It was very easy to cover oneself in billowing feathers, rings and masks. With a mask the face could become as wide as the shoulders. The desire to change shape reappears from time to time all through the history of costume: hats give height to the head, farthingales and crinolines transform the hips to wings. By altering his natural shape man showed his rejection of nature and his dominance over it. He re-made himself according to his own whims — and in his own image.

We can start to trace the history of clothes from the time when they began to be made of material, when they become washable and durable, capable of being changed to suit different occasions, and supple enough to be used in varying ways.

The first evidence we have dates from 3000 BC. A Sumerian terra cotta and a bas-relief in the Louvre show two women, one dressed in a loincloth, the other in what we would now call briefs. The rest of the body is naked, including that delicate part, the chest — which would

prove, if proof were needed, that people started to wear clothes to look attractive, not because they feared the weather. Both these garments are made of sheepskin and fastened round the waist with a padded belt. The loincloth probably came first and the briefs were invented by pulling the loose ends of the loincloth up between the thighs. From the loincloth, an open garment, and from briefs, a closed garment, two families of clothes emerged which were sometimes kept apart and sometimes worn together, and which survived throughout the history of costume, both in under and outer wear. But, underwear has not yet come into being at this time.

In Egypt during this period the slaves and the majority of the poorer people wore nothing, whereas the nobles were already using gold thread in their garments — first the loincloth, and then the tunic which also developed out of the loincloth by extending it downwards to the feet and upwards to the shoulders. A wide collar was sometimes added, again for ornament. Quite often men would wear false beards, and a prince would attach a lion's tail to the small of his back. Not only is man the master of his natural appearance, but his artifice need no longer be permanent, as with tattooing. He can change his clothes, return to nudity when he feels like it (modesty not yet existing), take off his beard, change his wig. From this time on change and movement are the chief characteristics of clothing — and fashion was born because man did not want to submit to any one of his self-created appearances, any more than to that given him by nature. To escape first from pre-destination and then from the conditions of his environment he insists on changing his form in order to have the eternal pleasure of rebirth. If an object is to supersede another it has to be of a more efficient shape or material than its predecessor. With clothes it is different: the fact that they are new is sufficient to give them precedence.

Only tradition halts this cult of metamorphosis: the transformation of costume is slow in times when the bases of thought and of society are stable. The evolution of Egyptian fashion can be traced in periods of several centuries, that of our own times in decades or even less.

Clothes soon took on a symbolic

value in ancient civilizations. The rank, power and competence of a man, as acknowledged by society, were shown in his dress. If it was only the slave who was suffered to go naked, this was because he represented nothing but himself. The length of a tunic, its colour, the movement of its folds were indications of caste. A man of high rank had the right to wear a loincloth under his tunic, and from this developed the underskirt, that is the first under-garment, and its development is due not to a sense of hygiene or fear of cold, but to a sense of social status. From the Middle Empire to the end of the nineteenth century clothing kept this function of indicating status, a function that was at times upheld by law or by custom.

In a theocratic society with an established hierarchy and a love of continuity, dress would not be expected to change except with serious crises of dynasty. In Egypt during the second millennium, and notably under the Rameses, both men's and women's clothes remained virtually unchanged. An upper class man would conduct his business in loincloth or underskirt, and put a tunic over the top when he was "dressed". His wife would normally wear two tunics, one of which became a chemise and was worn underneath. Transparent clothes were all the rage: both garments could be transparent, or just one, in which case it was usually the outer one, contrary to

R as-Shamra goddess, 19th-18th century BC: Ritual dress in traditional fabric (or fur) and bare breasts — there was still no sense of modesty about breasts or any other part of the body — clothes were not yet meant to conceal but rather to show the social class of the wearer.
Left: Maid servants — Rekhmira tomb, Thebes, 1500-1450 BC.

Musicians (Detail from Nakht tomb, Thebes 1422-1411 BC). Egyptian painters insisted on showing transparency, a characteristic of Egyptian clothes, although total nudity was reserved for children and slaves. Those who would have dared to have their own effigy nude would have risked being mistaken for commoners and would have completely lost their social status in the Other World.

present day fashion. The transparent effect was also obtained with revealing dresses of fine net.

Was there any sense of modesty at this time? It certainly did not apply to the breasts which many dresses left uncovered, and the rest of the body was not exactly concealed by the transparent clothes. The slaves, even those waiting at table, or admired as singers and musicians, were naked. Upper class women wore clothes to show their status, not to hide their physical charms.

A few slaves liberated themselves from the custom that expected them to be naked by wearing briefs much smaller than those of the Sumerians, a tiny embroidered *cache-sexe* that free women then would never have adopted, even as an under-garment. It is tempting to believe that these slaves had brought the briefs with them from their homeland on the other side of the Red Sea, from what we now call the Middle and Near East. One must even be cautious about supposing the Sumerian briefs had survived at all. During the last centuries of Sumerian civilization there was no article of clothing that resembled the briefs. There were tunics and loincloths, often transparent, and long shawls which sometimes covered the tunic almost completely, turning it into an under-garment as also happened in Egypt.

The observation that the first under-garments, which were chemises and underskirts, were originally outer garments that were covered over, applies not only to the Egyptians and the Sumerians, but also to the Assyrians, the Chaldeans and the Phoenicians. Another more general observation is that usually the outer garment was transparent. This means that the idea of an under-garment which is only seen by a privileged few and covered up by other clothes in public, did not yet exist. To dress was to exhibit one's wealth, hence the luxury of an outer garment that was either transparent or shorter than the under one.

What is most interesting among the peoples of the eastern Mediterranean is the mixture of sewn and draped clothes. Even the Egyptians who wore sewn dresses held up by shoulder-straps, wrapped loincloths round their bodies. From the time of the eighteenth dynasty onwards, draped dresses fastened simply with a knot at chest level, were in fashion. Eventually most outer-garments were sewn, and under-garments draped.

After the second millennium the lands between the Black Sea, the Caspian and the Red Sea were invaded by the Hittites, Persians and Indo-Europeans. The appearance of clothing of a closed kind in contrast to the open dresses of the ancient river valley dwellers, is more likely to be due to the influence of these invaders than to the survival of the Sumerian briefs.

The migrants had brought from the distant steppes trousers and breeches which were almost exclusively worn by men, whereas around the Black Sea the women seem to have adopted them. From the Persians the idea of wearing trousers spread to the Semitic peoples, so that in the second Book of Moses breeches are considered an essential part of priestly attire: "And thou shalt make them linen breeches to cover their nakedness; from the loins even unto the thighs they shall reach." (Exodus 28:42). It seems likely that in the Hebrew mind closed-system clothes which isolated the lower part of the body gained a religious and moral significance.

But in general this aversion to the flesh was not part of the Mediterranean nature which explains why, from the Egyptians to the Romans, they preferred open, flowing clothes — to the point where Egyptian women who had cold legs in winter, wore two "stockings" round their thighs, held up by a suspender-belt so as not to cover their private parts. The Indo-Europeans were not sophisticated enough in moral and religious matters to associate wearing closed trousers with an idea of purity. They probably invented them because they were better suited to their endless travels. Anyway, wherever they went they established the custom, from the Black Sea to the Atlantic and as far as Scandinavia.

If in the early centuries of the first millennuim we leave Egypt to take a look at the Mediterranean civiliza-

tions, we find in Etruscan and Aegean clothings themes with which we are familiar from the valleys of the Euphrates and the Nile. The Etruscans have nothing but open clothing; they alternate between being naked and dressed, are fond of transparent clothes, and drape shawls either next to the skin or over a dress that tends to become an under-garment.

Yet the Aegeans, of whom Crete is representative, show a preference for the curve which is completely foreign to Egypt. The Cretan skirt was wide and rounded. It flared out over hoops of rush and metal, and had additional flounces over the top.

These hoops are the first undergarments worn only by women. They prepare the way for the "bustles", "farthingales", "dress-improvers", "crinolines", "panniers" and "hooped petticoats" which briefly but frequently stand out in the history of underwear, as if at regular intervals, tired of being contained in a cylinder, women want to escape from nature and spread their hips wide.

Every time they widen the lower part of their bodies, women draw in the upper part, and whittle their waists with corsets in order to look more attractive, whether it is the time of Napoleon III, the Renaissance or Minoan Crete. The Cretan corset was laced, and opened wide in front, leaving the breasts bare, supporting them from underneath so as to press them upwards and outwards and show them to advantage.

Snake Goddess — Polychrome clay statue of Knossos, late Minoan period; ceremonial checked dress with flounces — close-fitting corselet with form-fitting midriff that enhanced a slim waist cinched by a rolled belt. The women of Crete invented the first two famous undergarments: the corset and the crinoline petticoat made with rush hoops and worn under flounced dresses.

In Crete we have found the first two specifically female undergarments — the crinoline and the corset. I do not know why some anthropologists have treated the Cretan women as chattels, assuming they were the spoil of raids throughout the Orient by drunken pirates. There is no reason to believe these women were not natives of Crete. Their evident sensuality makes them seem like playthings only to puritan eyes.

Of course we know so little about Cretan civilization that what we cannot deduce we have to imagine. The Cretan woman, made slender and rounded by her clothes, adorned by the medley of colours in her skirt and her make-up, is violently seductive. Does it matter whether she existed or whether the artists invented her? Her provocative form shows that to the Cretans women were exciting and enticing creatures: And we see for the first time that a wealth of extravagant underwear is linked with a period of intense sexual awareness.

The Greek civilization of the seventh century BC grew from the ruins of the Aegean, Hittite and Lydian civilizations, and at first it seemed like a regression. The only garment a Greek woman wore was a straight piece of cloth with neither seam nor hem. The Greeks' skill is only shown in the art with which they wore this simple cloth. The ways of varying dimensions and proportions offered innumerable aesthetic combinations. The inventiveness of the folds and the fall of the material led to two very similar styles, the Doric "peplos" and the Ionic "chiton" — the former plain and straight, with a clean line, rather like a Doric column, the latter more mannered, more decorative, like an Ionic column. The peplos was made of heavy wool and followed closely the line of the body; the chiton of fine material like linen, in a profusion of colours and delicately pleated in a way which suggested the female form rather than outlined it. Both garments could be either ankle- or knee-length. They

fastened on the shoulders with clasps, and the chiton covered the upper arms too; both dresses showed their origins in the shawl (one that hung from the shoulders, not one that was wrapped around, Asian style), and the chiton was open the length of the body on both sides. Then part of it was sewn up, and this combination of a sewn and draped garment was called a "closed chiton". Eventually it was fastened down to the waist in order to show off the figure better. Nothing was worn under the chiton, but in winter a woman wore a "himation" over it, that is a draped cloak made of a single piece of cloth. The Greek woman had no undergarment to draw in or curve out the chiton. It was draped with such care because its pleats had to remain in place without the assistance of a corset or hoop: under it the woman was naked.

From Athenian writings which criticize the immodesty of the Spartan girls, one might think the Greeks invented virtue. In their short opensided chitons the girls showed their bodies when they walked.

But writers who have judged the chasteness of the rest of Greece from the severity of the Athenians forgot that they disliked the Spartans and were inclined to judge them harshly. Moderation was another Athenian characteristic. What they reproached the Spartans for was not showing their bodies, but doing so too often. One might catch a glimpse of an Athenian woman's thighs or buttocks or breasts as she moved, but no more than that. She did undress publicly to bathe in one of the city fountains or in the sea, or for a religious festival, but her dignity was safeguarded because undressing on these occasions was never a gratuitous act.

This half-modesty of the Athenians knew nothing of the eastern Hebrew and Christian beliefs we have inherited which impose the idea that certain parts of the body are shameful. The Greeks did not cover themselves out of sexual morality, but out of love for civilization. These ardent city dwellers wanted to distinguish themselves from barbarians by having different costumes for different occasions, and nakedness counted as one of these costumes. Their love of beauty applied to their bodies as well as to the elaborately draped clothes they wore. One garment, the "chlamys" combined nakedness and clothing: it was a cape that an athlete wore next to his skin, leaving the right half of his body naked and covering the left in elaborate folds. Vases and bas-reliefs show that in combat or when crouching a Greek showed that part of his body which we keep the most hidden, without any embarrassment.

If further proof were needed that the Greeks' habits of dress were dictated simply by a love of beauty, one has only to remember that from the first invasion right up to the Dorian invasion the Greeks came to

Philomène, Procné and Itys, Attic bowl. Top: Atalanta — Attic bowl; a "brassiere" worn with a loincloth folded between the thighs — very similar to the structure of modern undergarments — exclusively used for sporting activities.

the Mediterranean wearing trousers, and that they abandoned these straight away for a free, flowing garment. Or better still, they were never tempted to imitate the Scythian slaves they employed as policemen and who wore trousers like the other Indo-European barbarians. The Athenians called them the "anaxyrides" and they were the lowest form of savagery. The mocking hatred of the Greek citizens for these poor policemen ridiculously attired in their anaxyrides foreshadows the conflict in dress which arose in the fifth century AD when the trousered barbarians conquered the toga-clad civilized races.

It is surprising that some ethnologists have attempted to base their theories on the supposed contrast between sewn and draped clothes. Sewn clothes conflict so little with draped that one finds the two combined. Greek dress was for centuries a combination of sewing and free folds which followed the contours of the body and changed with its movement. A draped garment is not altered because a seam replaces a brooch or a pin; a chiton sewn down the sides still moves just as freely. The significant and major contrast is between the draped-and-sewn garment and the sewn-and-fitted one worn by the barbarians and still worn by Western men today. This difference can never be reconciled.

It is the difference between an open and a closed system of dress.

The first respects the body's need for contact with the air, the second rejects it. It is the difference between a piece of cloth that moves freely with the shape, position and movements of the body it covers, and a prefabricated container which accentuates the crudely diagrammatic aspects of a man; the difference between the asymmetry of unequal and moving folds and the inert symmetry of the sheath with four protruding tubes which is modern man's dress as it has developed from the uniform of the Athenian police.

Another difference: the draped-and-sewn garment did not emphasize the distinction between the sexes. Men and women in Greece wore similar clothes, and the case of the poet who was so poor that he and his wife had only one tunic and so took it in turns to go out, has been quoted before. The distinction was created subtly by the shape of the body beneath the folds of the cloth.

It is not surprising that these differences are slight, because since the appearance of clothes, we have seen in Egypt and in the East that their purpose was to show social rather than sexual distinctions. However, among the Cretans, Persians and barbarian Indo-Europeans we have noted the beginning of a difference between male and female dress. This sexual distinction does not exist among the Greeks.

This anomaly can be explained by the Greeks' great chagrin that two sexes exist on earth and not just one. This treachery of nature left them inconsolable. Unable to do anything about it, they used uniformity of dress to prevent the Greek women from insolently exhibiting their femininity as the Cretans did, kept the young girls as well as their wives in seclusion, and turned to homosexuality.

Other people had built civilizations before the Greeks (I am thinking particularly of the Egyptians), but without knowing it. Greek civilization was the first in which the citizens were aware of what they were doing. This explains their open hatred for the barbarians, whether clever tribes from the east, or savages from the mountains and steppes to the north. It also accounts for their dislike of nature untamed and undomesticated. Because the instincts are part of our natural heritage they were repugnant to the Greeks — particularly the sexual instinct. The Greek was homosexual because he was undersexed. Love of static beauty was more important to him than the changing thrills of the senses He did not simply identify with truth and goodness, he absorbed them.

If, at other moments in history, clothing and architecture evolved together, this was not because of a conscious decision. I am convinced, however, that the Greeks who used cloth much as they used other materials, knew that the fluting of their columns was a transposition of the folds in their chitons. Since the earliest times there has been a parallel between the shape and contour of a clothed human being and a sculpted pillar. As early as the beginning of the sixth century BC the Samian

statue of Hera was a pillar comprising stylobate, fluting, drum and the beginning of a capital. Soon the column and the person became interchangeable — the Caryatids support the tribune of the Acropolis. But these women-pillars are never naked. They are always clad in fluted chitons, so that from a distance they can

be mistaken for men, thus participating — and for eternity, through the permanence of stone — in the myth of androgyny, which was overcome through the will of Zeus.

In such an environment it would have been out of place for women to exhibit their physical characteristics. Until the Hellenic period, that is the decline, sculpture as well as custom forbade the emphasizing of femininity. Women had to hide their breasts and hips. None of the under-garments that were so popular in Crete and Mycenae would have been tolerated in Classical Greece, for they were intended to thrust out the breasts, taper the waist and emphasize the hips. With neither corset nor crinoline, Greek women had to make do with underwear that was as plain and discreet as possible.

First they adopted the "apodesme", narrow bands of material which they wrapped beneath and round their breasts in order to support them. It was not intended to flatter the bosom but rather to flatten it, so that it did not move when they walked. Then the narrow bands of the apodesme became even narrower until they

were just a thin red ribbon that encircled the bust from their breasts to the waist. These were called "anamakhalisters" and "mastodetons".

With the usual perverseness that governs fashion, the narrow bands, tired of having become so thin, suddenly grew to the size of a scarf. By the Hellenic period it was sometimes transparent, for women were beginning to wonder whether they did not have a sexual role to play after all, and in his *Dialogues on Love* Plutarch proclaimed the death of Classical Greece by observing that in certain cases a girl could be the object of desire as well as a boy. At the same time more bands developed, called "zona", which wrapped round and flattened the stomach.

The Greeks were not inventors, they were discoverers. The mathematical, physical, judicial and artistic laws they arrived at were not considered as new things, but as ancient secrets which they came upon one by one. Plato, in this sense, is the most Greek of the philosophers. New clothes displeased them because they could not be linked with an old idea, but were utterly and brashly new. They resorted to invoking tradition to justify any change in clothing. They convinced themselves that the zona had been worn by men in earlier times, and that if nudity was now usual in the stadium it was because an athlete had once won a magnificent race in which he had lost his zona.

In the same way, when women

decided they preferred a linen tunic to the chiton or the peplos, they invented a legend which was echoed by Herodotus. The tunic was sewn on the shoulders instead of being fastened with a sharp-edged fibula, often in the shape of a hook or needle. It was claimed that the Athenian women had used these formidable weapons to tear into the body of a messenger bearing bad news — hence their suppression. In reality, the tunic had great advantages. It did not require the constant attention of one hand and arm to keep it up; it was made of a very fine material, pleated and fastened with a belt round the waist, and moved softly round the legs and covered the arms with its folds.

With the tunic the mixture of nakedness and dress which had characterized the clothes of the Classical era was at an end. Women disappeared under their clothes. The himation became longer and wider so that it could be wrapped around better, and a hood was added. The only part of the body not covered was the face. The terra cottas of Tanagra showing chilly ladies all muffled up, their modesty really inspired by coquetry, mark the end of a state of mind and a particular sensual awareness. The reign of a new woman has started; she is as seductive as the Cretan, but cleverer and more hypocritical. Under the himation which was carefully wrapped around her to arouse desire, she wore two

linen tunics. For a new under-tunic had been created, which through the centuries would produce the chemise and the slip. Under this smooth and sensuous garment the new Athenian wore bands or a scarf round her breasts and hips. It gave her a sensuality which the Dorian and Ionian women, with their bodies free under one piece of open cloth, had never felt. For the third-century Athenian woman, who never showed herself naked and did not even allow a glimpse of her body, nudity had assumed its erotic value. And to remind her that under her tunic she was vulnerable and accessible, she wore the bands of cloth round her breasts and hips, which in no way protected her, but made her conscious of the freedom of her body. Earlier on the evolution of costume in Greece signified the victory of a humanist dream over nature, but now nature was taking its revenge through the agency of the women.

THE LESSON
OF THE COURTESAN

From now on ladies' underwear is motivated by modesty and by licentiousness, either alternately or simultaneously. In Rome, where from the third century BC until the end of the Empire, underwear kept increasing in numbers and growing more and more complicated, it seems that at first it was decency, if not modesty that encouraged the bands of cloth like the Greeks had worn round their breasts and hips. In the heyday of the Roman Republic sensuality was so suspect that a respectable woman put on layers of underwear to cover herself from head to foot, and her tunic even had a broad flounce stitched onto the bottom so as not to compromise her reputation by allowing her heels to be seen — whilst the courtesans wore short and quite often transparent tunics.

Unlike the Greek women at the end of the fourth century and the beginning of the third who wrapped themselves in clothes to arouse desire, it seems that the Roman women started concealing their bodies out of

Flagellation of the initiates and the dancer, detail, House of the Mysteries — Pompei, end of 2nd century beginning of 1st century BC.
Left: Love's chastisement — Pompei.

Polymnie, Achilleon, Corfu; Roman statue wearing a classic Greek gown.

modesty. Even at the beginning of the Empire a tunic and a wealth of underwear were still associated with prudish reserve, and Ovid, preaching a greater freedom in matters of love, exclaimed: "Get away from me, you thin bands that proclaim virtue."

These bands, the successors of the apodesme, were called "taenia". They were worn under the breasts as in Athens. Small girls wore wider ones called "fascia" which covered the breasts and were intended to arrest their growth. When the damage was done (that is when the breasts had grown) a cruel leather "mamillare" was used to flatten and conceal them. It may be that at first this oppression of the rounded contours reflected, as in Greece, an obscure desire to make women mannish or at any rate to prevent them from emphasizing the characteristics of their sex. But since the Romans were much more inclined to normal love affairs than the Athenians and Spartans, it is probable that the mamillare and the fascia were worn as disciplinary measures rather than as a rebellion against natural inclinations. The pleasures of the flesh seduced the young men and enticed them away from their duty to serve the state, therefore it was necessary to render the female body as harmless as possible. It is no exaggeration to say that the chaste Roman's mistrust of the female body surpassed even that of the early doctors of the Church. And contained in that mistrust was a fear which constituted an act of homage such as would never have occurred to the Greeks.

We should not let ourselves be led astray by the cruelty of the mamillare. Very soon it was worn only by women whose bosoms were too generous for the fashionable conventions of the time. More common was the "strophium", a sort of scarf that was wrapped around the breasts to support them without suppressing them. At this time one finds different sorts of strophium all round the Mediterranean, notably the one with shoulder straps that Jewish women wore. The "capitium", a bigger and softer version of the strophium, was mostly worn by the lower classes.

The bands of the Greek zona lengthened to form a real girdle round the hips. The alternative garment was the "cestus", also of Greek origin, which enveloped the body from the breasts to the groin.

It is probable that the blossoming of underwear started for reasons of decency, but by the end of the second century the Romans obviously gave a lascivious value (of which the Greeks had been quite unaware) to the bands, scarves and embroideries that covered the more disturbing parts of the female body.

These beginnings of a fetish cult are also reflected in the popular phrase "zonam solvere" which meant to marry. The cestus, which according to legend was invented by Venus and offered by her to Juno, is seen by Martial as the trap from which no man can escape, as the lure that is always powerful enough to make the flame of love burn bright, as he himself is roused by contact with a cestus "still warm from Venus' fire".

Over these clinging underclothes the Roman woman wore a knee-length, sleeveless under-tunic. Often the capitium was worn over this tunic as the corset was worn over the chemise seventy years ago. The "cingulum", a belt which held up and draped a part of the dress, also went round the tunic. Women fastened it under the bosom, girls on the hips, which gave the adult and the adolescent a different profile. Lastly, before putting on her "palla", the Roman woman put on an underskirt called a "castula". This was soon to be held out by a little crinoline of wooden hoops similar to that of the Cretans, or perhaps derived from that of the Etruscans — or maybe it just happened spontaneously because of the need to widen their hips that women suddenly seem to feel.

Even if, in the street, a man and a woman still resemble each other in appearance, it is the underwear that differentiates her, marking the awareness of her sex, to the male's great satisfaction.

This does not mean that after Greece we have come upon a sexually balanced society. I have already said that in its muscular period the Roman Republic mistrusted women — not only in its laws, which always made them minors, but in its morals too. Custom required that a man should not desire his wife and should not involve her in a sensual affair. He was allowed to esteem her as a mother and a housekeeper, but if he were known to consult her on an important matter he would lose face. And wine was forbidden to women because they were supposed to be too excitable.

As always in such cases, practice softened the excesses of the rules and regulations. With old age many Roman wives became domestic tyrants. But this late reversal could not make up for the sober love-life of the Roman couple. To satisfy their sexual appetites the men turned to courtesans, having less inclination to homosexuality than the Greeks.

At first the courtesans were dirty, badly dressed little creatures, usually slaves, who lived in the gutter, offering themselves in their see-through tunics from half-open doorways. By the end of the second century they were an elite of elegant, perfumed, cultivated and ambitious adventuresses, whose insolent liberty contrasted with the docility and ignorance of the well-bred women.

In the first century BC Rome was an international city. Even if it still looked like a largish provincial village with hilly, narrow streets, it was nevertheless the capital of the Mediterranean, and however dingy it seemed after Athens and Alexandria,

Erato, Achilleon, Corfu; Roman statue wearing a typical classic Greek gown.

Isis, detail, marble statue from Pompei. Opposite: Veiled vestal virgin. From the 3rd century BC until the end of the Roman Empire, the prudish Roman girl progressively turns into a seductress, using all the underwear worn until then by Mediterranean women: Greek bandages, crinoline petticoats from Crete, Egyptian tunics and petticoats.

it welcomed cosmopolitan adventurers. Every day more courtesans arrived, who were born beside the Nile or the Orontes, grew up in the eastern ports and acquired worldly ways in Athens. They spoke all the languages of the Mediterranean and brought to Rome new depilatory creams, new lotions, new fragrances, new cookery recipes, cestuses with embroideries that had never been seen before, intriguing postures for making love, and the religions nurtured in Asia.

The Romans were initiated into the mysteries of Isis, whose altars were soon to triumph within the city as well as around it, in bed. By the end of the Republic, Rome had acquired so much power and perfection that it had become irksome. It had reached the stage other civilizations had reached or were to reach, where it could only continue by betraying itself. On the couches of the exotic courtesans, the top officials dreamed of replacing the old-fashioned, boorish gods by the enticing Asian deities with their new and licentious mysteries; of rejecting a majestic and meddlesome system of law for a smart new autocracy. So in the middle of the first century BC the Roman elite prepared to receive the religion of the Hebrews by welcoming those of their neighbours.

Not all the courtesans came from the other end of the world. Many, whether slaves or plebians, were born in Rome and some were influenced

by the marvellous foreign courtesans and introduced a new style into Roman ways; they were frivolous, capricious, superstitious and extravagant. The Romans also had the right to keep concubines in their own houses, lower class girls with whom they had the emotional relationships that decency forbade with their wives, and which they only got at a high price (both financially and emotionally) from the courtesans.

The first century BC is marked by woman's acquisition of power, not in a legal, but in a sensual and worldly sense. The courtesans and concubines were rivalled by a new set, the widows and divorcees. It was common for a child of seven to marry a man of thirty; this age difference produced a large number of young widows who could lead a free life, who were often rich and had much leisure to devote to the arts and to men. The Romans quite often married as much as three times, so divorcees were just as numerous, and usually the reputation of adultery that accompanied them predisposed them to amorous adventures. Even married women joined in the race, the more willingly because the harsh punishments they had once risked had been moderated.

By the first century Rome had quite modern ideas about sexual relationships, but only outside legal unions, in defiance of family ties, and solely through women who specialized in the arts of love, emotion and conversation. Their greatest asset was their beauty and so they lavished more care on their bodies than an honest woman would have considered justified. This explains the vogue for beauty lotions, dyes and rouges. While the virtuous wife thought of the bands she wore as under-garments designed to protect her modesty and assure her comfort, the courtesans, who won their battles in bed and who owed their power to intimacy, considered the strophium, underskirt and crinoline as effective weapons. They even invented a garter which they tied above the knee, where it was completely superfluous since stockings did not exist, and set it off with a jewel, a glittering invitation to desire.

After all, what the Roman courtesans invented on the eve of the great Christian debacle, was heterosexual love — and it badly needed to be invented. But it was still not complete. It was not until the second part of the Middle Ages, in France, that it became one of the highest functions of the soul and the intellect. In Rome it was only a desire pushed to its extreme. In a society where it was unseemly to lust after one's own wife, it was the courtesans' role to arouse and satisfy that appetite. Public morality which would not have tolerated a poet praising the shapeliness and attractiveness or the underwear of his wife, encouraged him on the other hand to paint this sort of picture if the heroine was a courte-

Polymnie, Roman statue wearing a typical Greek gown.

Ares and
Aphrodite, Pompei.

san. Catullus, Propertius, Tibullus and Ovid are a line of elegiac poets whose work was inspired largely by courtesans, and one or two well-known adulteresses.

What their work conveys primarily is that from the second century the Romans moved away from homosexuality. In Tibullus one finds serene allusions to short liaisons with a boy, and even a state poet like Virgil was not afraid to describe a homosexual couple in a sympathetic way. But these are only diversions, the old Greek infatuation has barely survived. This change came about through the violent and tumultuous passions that the courtesans' love affairs aroused in the Romans. They learned not only to enjoy the pangs of physical effort but also the anguished pleasures of jealousy. All at once, pederasty seemed rather silly — a sort of scouting they had outgrown. It was deemed perverse to love women, and they were mad about perversity. Ovid has admitted as much. He was not hostile to homosexuality, but he had to admit that it was too tranquil, too ordinary, and that it is not in the embrace of another man that a man can satisfy his tensions and desires, but in the arms of the stranger that is a woman. She is built differently, willing to be possessed completely, and always ready to betray, so there is all the more reason to try and keep her: the gift she makes of herself becomes important the moment one imagines someone else as the recipient.

Women understood very well that they could only become the objects of passion by exploiting and accentuating the natural differences that made them seem strange to men. Conservative in their outer clothes which were open to social censure, they let themselves go on under-clothes. They had to keep reminding their lovers that they were a different sex. They played the men's games, knew what men dreamed of, and made themselves extravagant to please them. It was not just the courtesans who applied themselves to this, but also, following their example, the respectable women who did not see why they should not become objects of desire too. Roman women began to experience a voluptuousness they had not known existed, any more than Greek women did.

A women of imperial Rome wore all the under-garments that the Mediterranean world had conceived since prehistory: bands and scarves from Greece; crinolines from Crete, tunics and underskirts from Egypt. It was a synthesis through opulence, much like the one we live in now. But still Rome respected the main points of the ethics and aesthetics of Mediterranean dress: for men and women alike it remained open and flowing.

Today a man done up in shirt, pants and trousers is not aware that he is naked underneath it all, yet if he gets out of the bath and puts on a bath robe, he is. After Brutus had stabbed him Caesar's last action before collapsing was to gather up his toga to cover the nakedness he was aware of under the linen folds. One cannot grasp the sensuality of the Ancients without understanding the extent to which men and women realized they were naked under their

clothes. This physical certainty delighted them.

But this delight was threatened by Semitic puritanism which discredited the joys of the flesh under the banner of Christianity, and by the barbarians at the sources of the Rhône and beyond the Rhine and the Danube who wore the close-fitting clothes of the orientals which better suited their arduous life.

By the first century of the Christian era the fate of the world hung on the outcome of struggle between the civilized southerners and the barbarians from the north, from the sea and from the eastern steppes — that is between a society in togas and a horde in trousers. We know that the Roman Empire collapsed under the double plot hatched for the one part on the banks of the Jordan, for the other on the banks of the Don and the Vistula. But its downfall was not due to battles lost in the field: it came about because the Romans betrayed themselves and admitted that their enemies were right. Their first mistake, small as it may seem in itself, was the adoption of clothes that enclosed the lower belly, thus conforming to the Hebrew barbarian's modesty and the Indo-European barbarian's concern for the practical. This new garment was called a "subligaculum", and it resembled the bikini-type suits shown in the mosaics of some of the Roman villas, notably the Villa Casale in Sicily. They were costumes worn for performing many sports, especially water sports, and consisted of a brassière and panty like those worn on the beach today, also like those worn by the Sumerian goddesses and the Egyptian slaves, and a bit like the garments of the Greek acrobats. Even though this costume shows the adoption of a closed system of dress, it would be wrong to suppose that it was widely worn. Later on there are many instances in western society of sportswear, theatrical outfits and even children's clothes being adopted by upper class society, but there is no evidence that the subligaculum was

A maidservant doing the hair of a young girl, painting from Herculanium.

worn by Roman matrons when they were bathing.

This subligaculum was the under-garment the Romans betrayed their way of life for: it was a piece of cloth which had one end fastened round the waist while the other went be-tween the legs. Sometimes it was longer, like drawers, and covered the thighs, to be fastened down with garters. At first it was only worn by acrobats and actresses, then slaves were made to wear one when they were going to do energetic work. The gymnasts copied them, and soon little girls and adolescents put on a subligaculum whenever they wanted to run about, or like Philoenis, Mar-tial's young heroine, were going off to play ball. Then the courtesans copied the clothes of the sportswomen and adolescents, and presumably the mid-dle class ladies eventually decided to get their own excitement in trying to

arouse desire by using the same weapons as the whores.

However the subligaculum did not become overwhelmingly popular, but remained a garment worn by people of a particular social status, or for certain gymnastic exercises. The men who had been duly appreciative of most of the new underwear, did not respond to the closed subligaculum which was foreign to their Latin sensuality.

Still, even if the bathing costume and the subligaculum were not a great success, they did leave their mark on the open-dress empire. They were accepted in spite of a principle that had governed the whole of Graeco-Roman antiquity, codified by Quintilian: *nec strangulet, nec fluat.* To my mind this betrayal of a national sensibility was as serious and as revealing as that which prompted the Roman intellectuals to praise the barbarians' purity, the better to condemn the supposed rot in their own civilization. It is significant that while the women were giving in to the subligaculum, brought by the slaves from the east and from Gaul, the army was throwing over its traditions and adopting the breeches and even the trousers of the mercenaries. Although still omnipotent, first century Rome was starting to show signs of being a conquered city. Her nerves were beginning to twitch before finally letting go.

In peacetime the Aztecs wore draped clothes, but at war they put on a fitting uniform, like a mechanic's overalls: so the ancient Mexicans were familiar with both categories of clothes, draped and fitted, whereas most races chose one of them. This situation is also found in the closing centuries of the Roman Empire. With the subligaculum under their tunics, the women were wearing both draped and fitted clothes and this new tradition continued until in the Middle Ages they relinquished their fitted underwear.

Although trousers were worn in the army many Romans wore them only in war, and kept to the toga the rest of the time. This inconsistency was also settled in the Middle Ages when the men stopped wearing robes altogether and changed to trousers. The confusion of dress at the end of the Roman Empire was such that it did not finally disappear until the eve of the Renaissance — at the trial of Joan of Arc.

Some writers have tried to explain the dominance of fitted over draped clothes in the west by the harshness of the European climate compared to that of the Mediterranean. They forget that the climate was the same for men and women, and women selected open clothes, even as far north as Lapland, where they have always worn dresses and never been tempted to copy men's trousers in spite of the extreme cold.

The first reason one thinks of for assuming that clothing evolved in a certain way is never the right one.

THE TWILIGHT OF
THE MIDDLE AGES

Because the first centuries of the Christian era resulted in the collapse of the Roman Empire, there is too great a tendency to look on them as decadent. The historians are a bit like readers of detective stories who start by reading the last page. They know that Rome was sacked, and so they see everything that stands out in its history as leading up to this disaster. Yet until the end of the third century Rome was still clever and beautiful.

Apart from one or two influences from Gaul, clothes only modified slightly, but they did become more elaborate. In the third century women still wore an under-tunic, the "subcula" next to the skin, then the "stola" or underskirt, often the "palla" which was fastened by two brooches on the shoulders, and sometimes an embroidered bodice. The economic crisis did not curb the opulence of clothes. The toga-clad men and women remained convinced that they ruled the world, while on the other side of the Danube, beyond the boundary of the Empire, the trousered barbarian hordes grew more vociferous and forceful. The Galilean barbarians paved the way for those from the north in the same way as the subligaculum had penetrated the Mediterranean uniformity of dress. In 376 when the Danube was crossed, the Empire entered and the frontier opened before the Visigoths, it was

45

Panel of an ivory
diptych, 5th century.
Right: Saint Marthe,
from Saint Lazarus tomb,
1170-1189.

not after a battle had been lost, but because the Emperor Valens, softened by Christianity, took pity on these hordes and opened his arms to them. It was the end of one world, the beginning of another.

The one that began was a mixture of dying refinement and astonishing savagery; it was crude and unpolished, and remained so until the end of the eleventh century. It took seven centuries to achieve balance and find an identity. The Dorian invasion between the twelfth and eleventh centuries BC created a similar vacuum in Greece. The term Middle Ages should only be applied to the period before the twelfth century, after this the expression "New Age" is more accurate, because a civilization appeared then that was in a large part original.

During the Middle Ages proper, people just about existed but no more. The conquered civilized man tried to get on with the barbarian conqueror. He, not knowing quite what to do, did everything, either successively or simultaneously. Sometimes he felt like killing, sometimes like talking and listening, he abolished Roman law or eagerly submitted to it, he built or destroyed in any way that took his fancy.

Civilization is a strong and burning sauce that is diluted, cooled down, and rendered tasteless by invasions; nowadays, revolutions have taken the place of invasions. It always happens the same way: the civiliza-

tion loses in quality what it gains in quantity. It takes time to recover the quality and advance beyond it, so that in the end a much greater number of people benefit from it. The first centuries of the Middle Ages were decadent for the civilized, but progressive for the barbarians. This double standard was well illustrated by contemporary costume.

We have already glimpsed the barbarians' costume on the Parthian and Scythian slaves who formed the Athenian police force. It is characterized by the dominance of fitted clothes, either "braies", or a combination of trunk-hose and puttees, or knee-breeches and hose. I will use the word "trousers" for this type of clinging and closed garment which was much disliked right round the Mediterranean.

The conflict between the northern barbarians and the civilized peoples caused a related controversy regarding the superiority of the toga or trousers. The solution was as uneasy a compromise as was the whole period of the Middle Ages. Basically what happened was that the Latins started to wear trousers under their robes and the barbarians a robe over their trousers. The latter considered the toga a mark of social success, a step towards imperial dignity. The robe signified culture, religion and administration; trousers work and bravery. From this time on men all over Europe relinquished flowing garments and adopted tubular ones. For a while the trousers were sufficiently hidden by the robe to count as underwear; then they became the outer garment that we know, as the gown got shorter and was opened in front to become our coat.

The barbarians had started to distinguish between the clothing of the sexes, because although all the men wore trousers, in very few tribes did the women imitate them. Apart from the barbarians beside the Black Sea who have already been mentioned, it seems that the Vandal women were the only other ones to wear trousers, or at least short trousers, a bit like present day bermudas. The Gallic, Scandinavian, Visigoth and Teuton women wore dresses, either long or short tunics, or a bodice and skirt. Underneath they wore nothing.

Yet medieval women showed some inclination to adopt trousers. In Byzantium they were worn by servant girls. In Germany and France aristocratic women are sometimes portrayed in long dresses, open wide in front showing their trousered legs. It is possible that by the fifth century women had decided to imitate men. It was a sensible move since trousers were practical for riding or for working in the fields and they also afforded protection against the sudden assaults that the men of the period were fond of. But the innovation was not only contrary to tradition, which has always been strong in women's clothing, it also came up against the vigilance of the Christian church which already saw any changes in women's clothing as evil.

So if some Gallo-Roman women, copying the Vandals, wore what the bishop Victor de Vita called "feminalia" — short trousers coming down to the knee — the fashion was not widely adopted, at least not in the towns. Women did adopt one new invention, however, which was of barbarian origin: stockings. These probably grew out of the different sorts of Celtic and Germanic leg bandages. There seemed a danger that the stockings would cover the thighs and meet to form trousers, but this did not in fact happen until the Renaissance.

In general, then, women wore two gowns, an outer one which was brightly coloured and slashed open at the sides, and an under-garment of a lighter material. The under-garment was only worn by the aristocrats under the Merovingians, and did not become universal until after Charlemagne. The only other under-garment was a band to support the breasts that was tied on to the underskirt.

Wearing two gowns, one over the other (the "bliaud", a long close-fitting tunic, and the "chainse", a linen under-garment) is reminiscent of ancient costume in the period before women came into their own. The disappearance of the numerous underclothes that Roman women wore means that elegance and artistry have suffered a setback, and also that

47

woman's position in relation to man has changed. Everything conspires to put an end to her voluptuousness. The hostility of Christianity to the flesh dictated that clothes should hide a woman's shape and her skin, and impose modesty as a pattern of behaviour. Women now wore a type of chemise if they bathed. The barbarians' boorishness did the rest. They did not go in for flirtation or suffering like the Latin poets. Layers of underwear demanded slow and delicate seduction leading eventually to the conquest. The barbarians wanted it to be short and sharp.

To some extent women reverted to what they had been in the fifth century BC — a painful necessity inflicted both by nature and by society — but they were also the object of those transient desires that could turn a gathering of ecclesiastics into an orgy. Easily undressed and kept in ignorance of pleasure, the only way women could escape from being a prey was to strive to get ahead in a man's world.

The Middle Ages was a period of transition, and although the more intelligent people could see where the transition had started, they did not know where it was leading. They had only one hope: to get back to the golden age, that is the Roman age. Few periods have wrought so much havoc or ravaged the past so much whilst esteeming it. The barbarian upstart dreamed of himself as a patrician, but it was only a dream. He had

forgotten what had made Rome, and so he only imitated the unimportant details with unthinking zeal.

They aped a fashion in ignorance of its origin, in the same way as the Carolingian administrators hid their crude inexperience behind one or two Latin phrases. Although the great ideas of Roman justice had been lost, respect for the jurist, the expert, remained. And so the Treaty of Verdun was drawn up in a dramatically modern way by hundreds of experts who, aided by plans showing absurd river boundaries, cut the new empire to paper shreds, almost before it was born. This treaty showed that the barbarians had the same trust in scribes as the ancients did, but the barbarian Christian scribe had forgotten that his predecessor's success was due to the existence of free men. If the new frontiers cut a rift through a family that lived on both banks of a river or weakened regions that suddenly lost their main town, or towns that were cut off from their hinterland, it was because man and land had become properties to be sold and bartered like objects. There were no more free men, only the oppressors and the oppressed.

During what I call the Middle Ages (from the fifth century to the twelfth) there was only one serious attempt to revive Roman civilization in anything more than a superficial way. This was done during the sixth century by Justinian in Byzantium. Thanks to him Roman law survived and for a century and a half was in force as far afield as northern Italy and North Africa. Historians love to disparage him; they try to forget that western law derives from the Justinian compilation. They even condemn him for burning Greek manuscripts and preventing the spread of the Greek language. Of course this is true, but it is also true that the last Greek statue was sculpted in 120 BC and that from the point of view of a practical politician Greece was now nothing but a sponge that soaked up oriental poison or was kicked about by northern barbarians. As Gautier observed, civilization needs porters who work in shifts — first the Egyptians, then the Greeks, then the Romans. The trouble is that in the Middle Ages there were no porters.

The Middle Ages was not just a night, as it has been called: it was a long twilight. It went on until a stable and new race emerged. As if the barbarian and Christian invasions had not dulled the Mediterranean civilization enough, the Semitic peoples invented Islam with its two fatal axioms: the first which wanted truth established once and for all in an irrefutable, unchangeable, way, the second which insisted that no art had the right to portray life.

The West was well out of it. In seven centuries they managed to add pagan rites, folklore and romanticism to the religion that had come from the desert and they repulsed the Arabs. To achieve civilization all

they needed was free men.

This was achieved in an indirect fashion in France at the end of the eleventh century. Men were born different; it was not yet necessary to proclaim that all men are born free and equal, as happened after the Revolution. This indicates considerable progress because for centuries they had been born nothing. A whole set of complicated rules and customs grew up, designed to balance powers, curb excesses and protect the individual by establishing local, professional and even religious rights. If the miracle happened in France it was because the kings and the people got on well, because with no frontiers to the north and the east the kings needed the support of the people.

This period from the end of the eleventh century to the end of the fifteenth century should really be called the Renaissance, or even the birth of society. But since the period that started in the fourth century is called the Middle Ages, I propose to call the one that follows it the New Age. Even if historians do not consider the eleventh century as the meeting of two eras, the professors of literature do. Although they still call it the Middle Ages out of habit, they at least separate the four centuries that mark the start of French literature. Before this there was nothing, but from the eleventh century onwards there are the *chansons de geste,* the fables, the mysteries and the courtly romances.

A wedding —
Illustrated letter, Laon, 13th century.
<u>Left</u>: "Virtuous" statue from the Cathedral of Strasbourg, 13th century.

Coltres de sim e lane.

...cea de p...br ulr mannis et fiiſ
...conter calorem. noctm̄ine amentib; caloꝛe
...eſt uelbꝯ lineis ſubtnis eos.

T H E T W O
S E X E S

The New Age, this period that started at the end of the eleventh century, was not only marked by the birth of French literature, but also by additional activities like the Crusades, the birth of patriotism, the organizing of trade guilds, and in architecture the blossoming of Romanesque and the budding of Gothic. The whole period constitutes a historical unity.

During these four centuries both men and women, who until then had worn nightclothes and who were to wear them again later, slept in the nude. It would be absurd to attribute Chartres or the *Roman de la Rose* to the way people slept, but not less absurd to refuse clothing a significant place in the understanding of this civilization.

Until the eleventh century a nightshirt had been worn almost without exception. The Greeks started by keeping on their tunic when they went to bed. When they wore two tunics they kept the under one on at night. It was probably the

51

Romans with their constant attention to clean linen who first kept some tunics specially for nightwear. Eventually they must have been made slightly differently, because by the Carolingian period they were listed separately in trousseaux.

The sudden disappearance of the nightshirt has no material explanation. It did not coincide with a crisis in the manufacture of textiles (quite the reverse in fact), and to maintain, as has been done, that nightwear reappeared in the Renaissance because it protected the body from cold, is to suppose that Europe suddenly got unusually warm in the eleventh century.

I will take this opportunity to emphasize the futility of applying reasons of warmth to women's outer clothes as well as underclothes. Most women today believe they wear a slip to protect them from the cold, but they wear it from force of habit. In winter they are cold in nylon stockings but never question the need to wear them. And if, from time to time, boots which enable them to brave the cold, come into fashion, they disappear again as quickly although the climate stays the same. The styles and materials of underwear, less open to social stricture than outer clothes, can never be justified as functional. They are elements of civilization as unforeseeable as painting or poetry.

Perhaps I should explain my interpretation of the word "underwear" since I use it to include nightwear. I have extended its meaning beyond the usual etymological one. By underwear I mean a garment, which, either because it is hidden under another, or because it is only worn on certain occasions and in front of certain privileged people, cannot be seen, at least not entirely, by just anybody. This definition leads me to include with underwear not only night attire, but also bathing and dance costumes. I feel this is justified because the evolution of these different costumes is closer to that of underwear than to day-wear, both in spirit and in style.

The mystery of the disappearance

of nightshirts for over 400 years can be solved only by studying contemporary ideas about life, and particularly about sex. They had already changed considerably during the time nightwear was evolving. The early part of the Middle Ages was a confused jumble of remnants of civilization and new barbarianism, but after the eleventh century the western world suddenly seemed to grow up and stopped being surprised at the

existence of women. They discovered that relationships between the sexes are one of the most important problems of life, and in an effort to come to terms with this, distinguished very clearly between men and women.

Whilst literature set about exploring the psychological nuances that show men and women are different and not just unequal, dress started to illustrate the physical side of this phenomenon. In short, the Middle Ages added sex to costume. Until then, this had either not been done at all, or only in minute distinctions. Since then, the separate types of clothing have been maintained.

Details in women's fashion were often contradictory during the Middle Ages. Dresses were sometimes long, sometimes short. The female profile of the twelfth century — rounded breasts and wide hips — is not the same as that of the thirteenth century — higher breasts and accentuated waist — but some things did not change. In spite of one or two short-lived regressions, dresses grew longer and stayed that way. Women wore dresses in such a way that the part of the body that characterized them was revealed as if they had been naked, and that part was considered to be the stomach. Everything was arranged so that the curves of a woman's stomach, both convex and concave at the same time, should be emphasized by her clothes — to the extent that the hollow of navel should be discernible through the filmy cloth.

The number of under-garments had increased substantially since the Carolingian era. The "doublet", a short bodice in the tradition of the capitium, which announced the re-

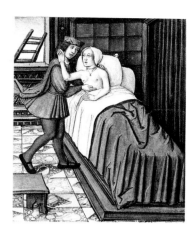

Lucretius, *The Life of Famous Women* Antoine du Four, 1505. Left: The bloody wedding night of the fifty Danaides with their fifty second cousins, *The Heroides*, Ovide, 15th century. In the Middle Ages, wearing a nightgown was just as significant as taking it off. Keeping one's nightgown on was one way to reject a sexual proposal. This is the case in 49 of those Danaides who are not at all interested in this conjugal relationship. The husbands are completely naked.

Seated woman,
Roman de la Rose —
Guillaume de Loris —
14th century. Going to
bed was a ceremony in
itself: the dress and the
underclothes were hung
on a horizontal pole and
the day slip was taken off
only when in bed.
<u>Below</u>: February, detail.
'*The Very Rich Hours of
the Duke of Berry*, 14th
century. "By underclothes
I mean those garments
that can only be seen by
some privileged person."

vival of the corset, was worn between
the chainse and the bliaud. The
small bands were back to support and
contain the breasts. They were worn
over the chainse which was now
called a *robe linge*, eventually to be
called a chemise. One sort of doublet
ended up by being worn over the
dress and thus became an outer
garment, the other continued to be
worn over the chemise. The medieval passion for underwear also produced the "gipon"; a close-fitting
waistcoat often worn over the dress,
but which fulfilled the role of a
corset, flattening the breasts to set off
the stomach which fascinated the
Middle Ages as the monument of
femininity.

Clothing was further complicated
by the *futaine*, a waistband; the
blanchet, a long camisole that took its
name from its colour; the *cotte*, a
short tunic with wide sleeves, which
because it laced up bore a slight
resemblance to the corset. In addition, the chemise had small pockets
filled with wadding that widened the
hips and thereby noticeably empha-

sized the lower part of the body.

These pads, like the bands and the
lacing, were intended to deceive, to
assist in creating an impression that
did not correspond to reality, but in
such a way that faced with a clothed
woman, a man might well get the
impression that naked, she would
still be the shape her clothing suggested. These under-garments are in
themselves meant to be unnoticed,
and their function is to make an
artificial shape seem real, so we will
call them deceptive underclothes.

The one constant factor in
medieval development was that
women's clothes became long and
increased in number, layer upon
layer. During this same period men's
clothes got shorter, and between the
eleventh century and the end of the

fourteenth century the masculine robe died completely. The different sorts of braiers, braies and trunk-hose combined to produce clinging trousers. And so the sexualization of clothes was achieved: men still wear trousers, and women dresses.

This break occurs only in Western Europe. The Byzantine men kept to the long gown all through the Middle Ages, which was partly responsible for giving them a reputation for effeminacy in France. All around the Mediterranean the asexual costume remained totally unchanged; men and women both went naked under their draped clothes. Then, most probably under Turkish influence, trousers spread — for women.

The European colonists of the nineteenth century were particularly conscious of the strangeness of races where the difference between men's and women's clothes is the inverse of our own. In their flowing robes the Muslims' gestures and movements seem very feminine to us as well, and they even squat down to relieve themselves.

Although many societies did not distinguish between men's and women's clothes, those that did often did so in opposite ways. The Muslims were not the only ones to dress women in trousers, it was the same in China, so that at the beginning of this century when the Chinese women wanted to assert their rights by making themselves mannish, the only way to do it was to give up

trousers and start wearing tunics. Today Europeans not only consider the dress as an inherently feminine garment, but also find it quite logical and functional that this should be so. Oriental critics did not have much

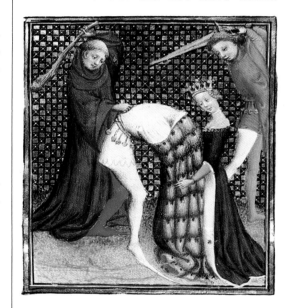

difficulty in showing that if one is talking about logic, protective trousers are better suited to women who are by nature on the defensive, than to men who are on the offensive.

By depriving men of robes and allowing them only for women, the Middle Ages was not obeying reason. What was wanted more than anything was to differentiate between the sexes, and it was done in this way because they followed the trend that had started with the big invasions. The braies that the barbarians brought were quite readily adopted by men to go under their tunics, particularly by farmers and soldiers. So breeches assumed a war-like, not to

Boccace, Duke of Berry, around 1410. "Reserving the use of gowns exclusively for women, which was greatly desired during the Middle Ages, marks a clear distinction between the sexes".
Below: Underwear for men, *Anatomy*, Gui de Pavie, beginning of 19th century. The *chausses* or knee breeches that covered the feet and the legs used to be quite short in the 7th century. They became higher as mens' clothes become shorter (up to the crotch). The high *chausses* are tied to the belt by laces. During the 14th century *chausses* did not stop at the crotch, but became long closed underpants which paved the way for the modern mens' suit.

mention a roisterous significance, which appealed to men during this period of chivalry, whereas calmer, quieter beings like women, priests, magistrates and officials showed their temperament by keeping to the traditional robe.

No period has attached so much importance to designating each class, each trade even, by a particular uniform as the Middle Ages did. It is hardly an exaggeration to say that everyone was in in uniform except the soldiers. They also considered it important that men and women should indicate their sexual differences in addition to differences of class. As we have seen this stemmed from their discovery that men and women are strangers to each other and that there can only be a dialogue between them once the differences, emphasized by every available means, have been accepted.

This dialogue preoccupied the Middle Ages. Courtly literature opposes immediate contact and stresses the slowness and difficulty of the conquest. The two strangers may only overcome the difference that separate them one by one. This is the theme of the *Roman de la Rose*. Neither Antiquity nor the early Middle Ages seem aware of the first approach, the first grasping of hands, the slow growth of a feeling shared or not, the progression from the first look to ultimate possession as essential steps in the game of love. This new approach, used by classicists, romanticists and modernists, was discovered by the New Age and immediately bewitched it. Seignobos' remark about "love, that invention of the Middle Ages" cannot be bettered. It is presented as full of difficulties, thwarted by the nature of things as well as by individual destiny. It is a series of trials that the man, and the women too, have to challenge and eventually conquer. Both the difficulties and the delights of achieving harmony are a result of the fact that man's nature is so different from woman's.

It is easy to see what role a woman's clothes played in this game of love; invasion was easy because she wore a dress, but so was defence because of her many underclothes.

In addition to those I have mentioned there were hose made of thread or wool, held up by garters above the knee, corsets which grew longer and were adorned with collarettes and gorgets of fine muslin, and then there was the girdle or "tassel". By the fifteenth century, although the décolleté left bare the shoulders and most of the breasts, dresses got longer and longer and trailed behind a woman as she walked, so that unless she had a page-boy, she had to use a *troussoir* — an iron hook attached to a cord, from which the train hung.

The *troussoir* aroused the imagination of the poets as much as the corset did. All lingerie that is worn next to the female body stimulates

Maulgis and Ysanne in the Queen's bedroom, Loyset Liedet, Renaud de Montauban, 15th century. The chemise, revealed at the deeply scooped neck and at the wrists, is made of a very thin transparent fabric, of a gold or saffron colour which was fashionable at the time. The quality of the fabric would differentiate the chemises worn by poor people from those worn by the rich. There was no class differentiation in the cutting itself, chemises were very simple, T-shaped and most commonly made of flax. Cotton, which was reserved for padding, will be used much later for underwear.

male inspiration, particularly transparent clothes. Yellow, gold and cream-coloured transparent materials were all the rage, particularly for making chemises. A woman wearing these was dressed and naked at the same time, and easily aroused a man's passionate desires.

The taste for underclothes themselves, in other words, fetishism, started in the Middle Ages, and was a new development in the evolution of sensibility. The garter in particular acquired an erotic value which it kept until the beginning of the twentieth century. The Duchess of Orleans, in the fifteenth century, had her goldsmith decorate her garter with sixteen enamelled conceits. Soon after, Rabelais wrote of the licentious behaviour of the elegant women of *Thélème* which led them to match their garters with their bracelets. The importance of clothes as an obstacle in the conquest, and also as a token of victory is borne but by the ladies' custom of offering one of their sleeves to the favourite suitor — a gesture it was quite easy to perform since sleeves were separate from the dresses and they had large collections of them. But the gift caused them some trouble because fashion demanded that arms should always be covered.

A concept of love that insisted to such an extent on all that distinguished between the sexes morally, physically and therefore in clothing, also demanded they should be naked in bed. It is the only explanation for the disappearance of the nightshirt.

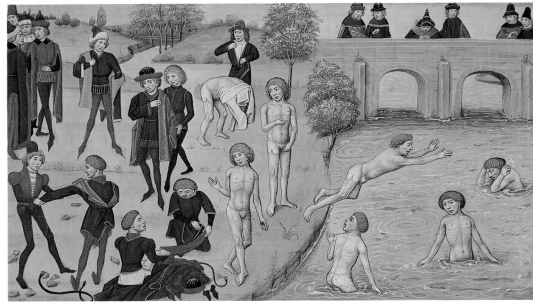

After all the care given to distinguishing clothes, it would have been a contradiction for men and women to look the same the moment they went to bed together — and nightshirts were identical for both sexes. Either new and different nightwear had to be invented, or they had to recourse to natural differences. Nudity was also the ideal solution because after the long series of obstacles had been overcome, it symbolized the end of the trials, the removal of any hindrance, ultimate victory.

Wearing a nightshirt in the Middle Ages had just as much significance as not wearing one. Conscious of his mistress's wishes, Lancelot kept his shirt on in bed, thus indicating that he had decided to resist her. The association of ideas between leaving off nightshirts and love-making was so great that "to sleep naked" meant to make love. In the sixteenth century when people again wore nightshirts, the wedding ceremony still demanded that the newly-weds should sleep naked on the first night. And for a long time the sceptical phrase: "a promise like that is as much good as married women who would go to bed in a nightshirt" was current.

When preparing for bed, a woman took off her dress and layers of underwear and put them on a hanger. She kept on her chemise until she was in bed and then slipped it under the bolster. There are many contem-

porary sources for these small details of private life, not only those that dramatize and sublimate love, but a whole literature that describes the daily routine of a couple with realism — because the Middle Ages had a passion for all aspects of sexual relationships, both trivial and idyllic.

When trying Joan of Arc for witchcraft her accusers brought for-

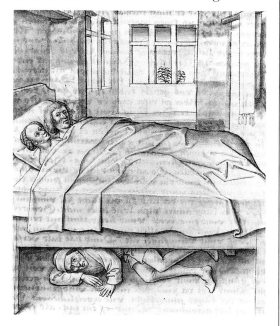

ward as serious evidence the fact that she had worn men's clothes. Joan's rebellion undermined the very basis of the medieval spirit which consisted of a naive confidence in the discoursive classification that distinguished and enumerated kinds of sins, their causes, effects and symbols. Medieval man had seven standpoints from which he examined sin, amplified by fourteen subdivisions and six spiritual weaknesses that were disposed to evil — not to mention the

four ultimate purposes and the eight truths that authorized the murder of a tyrant. In the midst of these systematic subdivisions the Middle Ages revered the man-woman duality.

At this time the visual sense predominated, and so it was differences in clothing and physical appearance that attracted the attention, which explains the scandal caused by Joan of Arc's mannish clothes and behaviour. They were contrary to the ethics and aesthetics of a period preoccupied with bisexualism to the point where behind the ramparts of dying Byzantium they quarrelled about the sex of the angels. But the Renaissance was approaching, and already in the bathing establishments of Paris the geishas who amused the clients were making way for the fairies, a revival of imperial Rome.

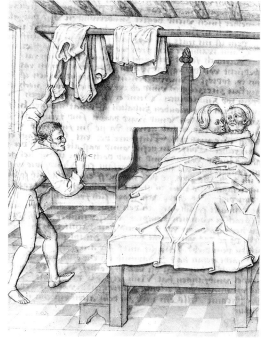

Portrait of Joan of Arc, Franco-Flemish School, 15th century.
Left: Two scenes representing surprised lovers, Bidjaii Fables, 15th century.

CATHERINE'S DRAWERS

It was the half secret, half openly declared intention of the Renaissance to destroy the rigorous distinction between the sexes made by the Middle Ages. There were three lines of attack. The farthingale created women bearing no resemblance to their predecessors who had fascinated the Middle Ages by revealing the feminine attributes of their stomachs through their clinging dresses. The wide unnatural hips of the farthingale made the rise and fall of the stomach disappear. That done, men and women went back to wearing identical nightshirts which hid their difference. Finally, by claiming the right to wear trousers, women tried to disrupt the system of dissimilar dress which had existed for nearly three centuries.

The Renaissance was a time of confusion, including sexual confusion. At the ecumenical moment when the Old Testament adapted itself to Greek mythology and the Evangelists came to terms with the Latin free-thinkers, it was to be

Venetian courtesan, after A. Fabric, 1593. Drawers made of a rich fabric and padded. The projecting bodice was known as a *panseron*.
Left: "Lady rising and dressing", by T. Dubreuil, 16th century.

61

"Gabrielle
d'Estrées and the Duchess
de Villars". French school,
16th century.

expected that artistic morphology would reflect the changes. Painters and sculptors put female breasts on men's torsos, slipped young men's glances under a madonna's eyelids, cultivated an ambiguity which could no longer pass for primitive since it followed on a time when sexes had been forced into visual separation.

This clear distinction disappeared in the first flush of the Renaissance. Inferior at the time of Charlemagne, different at the end of the Middle Ages, women now claimed equality. The two clearly defined sexes of the Middle Ages merged, and the gulf that had separated them was closed by the beginning of the sixteenth century. Homosexual tendencies marked both male and female dress.

By the sixteenth century women were prepared to make love to their brothers, or one of their women friends, to a swan like Leda did, or to a tramp who offered chance excitement. As free as men, they could know as much Greek or law as they did, rule a country, shoot a crossbow, write poetry, ride, hunt, and fornicate all over the place.

Drawers

It is said that it was Catherine de Medici who introduced women to trousers, called "drawers". These tied round the waist and covered the thighs down to the knees, there fastened to the stockings with garters.

It has been suggested that Catherine de Medici and her friends got the idea for drawers from the breeches that some peasant women were still

wearing, but it is easier to admit that they borrowed them from men's clothes. Men's trousers came into existence when the different sorts of breeches that had been undergarments became outer garments while the robe grew shorter and finally disappeared. With their drawers women intended to go back to the same costume as men, and destroy the distinction established in the Middle Ages between the dress as a feminine symbol and trousers as a masculine one

The spirit of the Renaissance was such that if it had not been slowed down and finally halted by the Reformation and then the Counter-Reformation, dresses would have been abandoned in the sixteenth century just as men's robes were in the Middle Ages, drawers would have become outer clothes — in short, men and women would again have been dressed alike. But whilst the literary phase of the Middle Ages lasted four centuries, the Renaissance did not even last a hundred years, a fact one tends to forget because of its far-reaching influence on the following centuries, like one forgets that even this influence was censored and expurgated at quite an early date. Women's claims to equality were over before the end of the sixteenth century, having aroused men's suspicion and vigilance. Molière made fun of them in his plays *Les Précieuses Ridicules* and *Les Femmes Savantes.*

Catherine and her companions needed an excuse for violating the taboo that demanded different dress

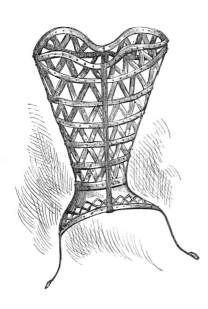

for each sex, and taking to men's clothes. They found it in a new way of mounting a horse. Instead of sitting on the saddle with their feet on a small board, they adopted the manner that has survived until today, of riding with one thigh horizontal, supported by a saddlebow. This position left their knees uncovered, so they could claim they had to wear drawers for the sake of decency. This reason, which is eagerly upheld by costume historians, is not really valid, for when drawers disappeared in the seventeenth century women still continued to mount in the same way in their dresses. The horse-riding excuse is even less valid because women often rode without wearing drawers, although they put them on unnecessarily on many other occasions — the courtesans wore them for walking in the street and took good care that everyone knew it.

Although drawers were underclothes, they. were intended to be seen as much as they were hidden. The Renaissance was a time when women paraded their legs. They showed them when riding, hunting, sitting in an armchair, going downstairs, taking part in sports and dancing. Their desire to show them is confirmed by their concern to have stockings and drawers that fitted perfectly.

If further proof is needed that women wanted to show off their legs, it can be found in the sudden transformation of drawers into a garment

skilfully padded out with satin to enhance the thighs and buttocks. It is also likely that they were open, for Brantôme relates how some women gave themselves to their lovers without taking off their drawers and so

kept them under an illusion about their figure.

At first drawers were· made of cotton or fustian, materials which were normally used for underclothes. But the women's desire to transform them to outer garments and give up their dresses meant that they were soon made of other materials: brocades and gold and silver cloth. Why did they fail?

The arrival of drawers was first justified for practical reasons (horse-riding) and on moral grounds (modesty) in the same way that today the most absurd fashions are recommended as being "natural". Some men were taken in and one was so duped that he actually praised women's integrity. "Women have started to wear some sort of breeches called drawers, out of concern for propriety. In addition to helping them keep clean, and protecting them from the cold, they prevent their thighs being seen if they fall off a horse. These drawers also protect them against adventurous young men, because if they slip their hands under their skirts they can't touch their skin at all!" This reasoning seemed plausible at first, and among the middle classes, who were the most concerned with respectability, mothers made their daughters wear drawers out of modesty — besides they did at first seem to fit in with the trend of the previous century to increase the number of women's underclothes. But it soon became obvious that drawers were intended to exhibit rather than to hide, when the allegedly modest ladies revealed their legs clad in gold and adorned with lace, precious stones and embroidery. Even the naïve writer I have just quoted began to wonder whether drawers were not "intended to attract the dissolute rather than afford protection against their impudence". The Reformation and the Counter-Reformation were of the same opinion. Slowly people began to realize that far from being chaste, drawers were evil, and that they had been adopted at court simply because

the ladies wanted to be able to hoist up their dresses freely, while waiting to abandon them altogether.

It was clear too that this movement towards masculinity was not unequivocal; at a time when men were interested in other men, it was an attempt on the part of the women to attract their attention *slyly* by making their thighs look like those of page-boys. For this strategy to succeed the spirit of the Renaissance would have had to last much longer, but it was crumbling before the end of the sixteenth century — and drawers with it.

Drawers had never been universally accepted. Their success with the upper classes in Italy and France had never spread to England or Germany.

Even the French aristocrats did not wear drawers all the time. In his *Histoires* Brantôme always specified whether or not his heroine wore drawers. This alternation almost certainly gave women a heightened sensual awareness of their bodies between the knee and the waist. Sometimes bare, sometimes covered, both states had a positive value, and women were very conscious of wearing or not wearing drawers, particularly because the farthingale left a large amount of free space around the lower part of their bodies.

The Farthingale

The farthingale was the name given to an assortment of pads, whalebones, iron wire, sometimes

Adjusting a "French style" farthingale, Holland, 1595. The farthingale was fashionable in Spain at the end of the 15th century and was introduced into France early in the following century. It was originally a stiff bell-shaped underskirt held up by wooden hoops which allowed it to drape down from the waist with no intervening folds. The French style replaced it by a circular pad by which the fullness of the skirt was evenly spread around the body while allowing for folds and pleats. Towards the end of the 16th century, a third type of farthingale appeared: a flat circular surface projecting at an angle, usually covered by gathered flounces, over which the dress could be evenly spread.

wood or wicker-work which fastened round the waist and spread skirts out in a huge curve.

It was a creative, not a deceptive under-garment. The wearer was not trying to make anyone believe that nature had given her hips as wide as her body was long and standing out from it at right angles. The farthingale created a new shape. It was completely contrary to the efforts of the Middle Ages which, even while employing artifice, had made woman's shape as natural as possible. The Middle Ages had moulded the stomach, and the Renaissance banished it beneath the enormous skirt that curved out over the farthingale. So at the time women took to wearing drawers on the pretext that they were sporting, they also encumbered themselves with a clumsy garment that hampered their movements in every way. Although they claimed to be covering their thighs as a protection against unsolicited caresses, they grew very fond of this contraption that held their dresses and under-clothes away from their bodies, thus making advances easier. The width of the garment can be gathered from this verse:

Alas, poor verdingales must lie
in the streete,
To house them no doore in the
citee made meete,
Syns at our narrow doores they
in cannot win,
Send them to Oxforde, at
Brodegates to get in.

These contradictions should put us on our guard once more against any logical explanation of fashion. To explain the folly of the farthingale one has to look for reasons in widely differing areas of sensibility. At the time of Renaissance the riches of the upper classes were reflected in their luxurious materials, and out of vanity, the women sought a way to show off their clothes as much as possible. But this lack of reticence, this os-

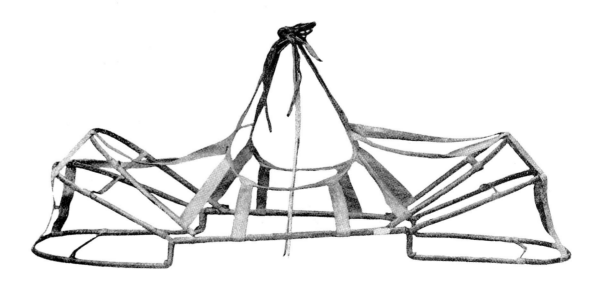

tentation, was less tied to richness itself than to the uses made of it, to an awareness of opulence. This awareness which developed as a reaction to the medieval cult of modesty and heroism, did not lead to bad taste in clothes (if by bad taste we mean excess), except in so far as this excess was characteristic of the times and was found in architecture, furnishings and jewellery as well. It is tempting to compare the medieval dress to the slender gothic spires, and the rectangular, over-decorated dresses of the sixteenth century to the heavy Renaissance windows, in the same way that one could distinguish between the Greek chitons that reflected the Doric and Ionic order.

The farthingale shaped the amplitude of the lower half of a woman's body and balanced this above the waist by the equally artificial volume created by the *basquine*. In these under-garments, woman's shape became completely unnatural, from shoulders to toes.

The Basquine

The medieval corset left the breasts bare, and hollowed the small of the back to emphasize the stomach. When the corset became the *basquine* it deformed the upper part of the body in the same way as the farthingale did the lower part. It was made of stiff cloth and fitted tightly over the waist, then opened out like a funnel, hiding the breasts under an artificial front over which the dress fitted. The

farthingale hid the femininity of the stomach and buttocks and the *basquine* the rounded soft line of the bust. The new being that the Renaissance created out of the medieval woman by inventing three under-garments (drawers, farthingale and *basquine*), represented the contem-

porary taste for rejecting old shapes, illustrated the preoccupation with all forms of artifice and typified the sexual unrest of a time when women dreamed of wearing trousers, and men of wearing the farthingale.

Consciousness of the break with the past was so strong that sculptors and stained glass artists who, in the medieval churches had portrayed the Virgin in the clothes of the period, dared not in the Renaissance show her in drawers and farthingale. It was the beginning of an era that concentrated on the notion of progress and the cult of anything new, so much so that great anxiety arose about the permanence of anything created, and religious art no longer dared seek inspiration in contemporary forms.

The Struggle for the Breeches. French school, early 17th century. This theme is found, always in the form of a caricature, until the close of the 18th century. It can be interpreted as woman's struggle to attain a social status symbolised by this specifically male item of clothing and consequently representative of male dominance.

PANNIERS AND BARE BOTTOMS

North of the Alps, supporters of the Reformation and Counter-Reformation had banished the excesses of the Renaissance, particularly in dress — drawers, farthingales, basquines were described as "devilish trifles". In spite of the attempted infiltration of Italian and then Spanish fashions, the seventeenth-century dress tended toward discretion. Everything favoured this, from the reign of the moralists to the introduction of the bourgeoisie into the ruling class.

After Malherbe, Sully and Charron, extravagance was no longer fashionable. Only excesses of reason were permitted from now on. The concept of state was rationalized for the first time, and the *Académie Française* was set up to rationalize even the language. If the language it used may seem excessive to us, we should still not forget this primary aim, indeed, to regulate language itself. Likewise architects were persuaded to seek inspiration only in symmetry, ba-

Lady of quality in full dress, wearing bodice and panniers, by Voizard, after Desrais, Galerie des Modes, 1778.
Left: *The Rising of Fanchon*, Lepicié, 18th century.

lance and clarity. Gables, projecting turrets and overhanging roofs disappeared at the same time as women's hips. It was the death of the farthingale, which persisted only in countries like Spain.

nied Mlle de Fontanges to her apartments. She was in a very gay mood and was telling her lover jokes about the diversion created when one of the ladies of the party fell off her horse. The king was laughing heartily ...".

In the seventeenth century men were men and women women; the former wore breeches, the latter dresses. The problem had been settled. Drawers disappeared. A few ladies still wore them for riding, but usually a skirt was considered sufficient.

Until the end of the eighteenth century, this basic nakedness gave rise to a number of accidents that were greeted with ribaldry. Bussy-Rabutin relates that "after hunting the king dismounted and accompa-

Louis XIV was similarly amused by a fall of Mlle de la Fayette. Many writers became infatuated with the subject, among them Voiture:

Et mon coeur autrefois superbe
Humble se rendit à l'amour
Quand il vit votre cul sur l'herbe
Faire honte aux rayons du jour.

The ladies smirked and threatened to go back to wearing drawers to punish the men for their lechery. The Compte de Caylus, amused by the agitation of the ladies, told them it was quite right that everyone should benefit from the sight of a "happy fall" and refused to provide drawers unless he himself was allowed to fit them:

Du moins faut-il bien que je sache
Ce dont il est question
Et j'y mets la condition
De me montrer ce qu'on veut que je cache.

Occasionally a fall had an unexpected outcome. In the *Mémoires du Chevalier de Gramont* we learn how, thanks to a tumble, Miss Churchill seduced a Duke into marrying her, although she was very ugly indeed. Hamilton describes the incident with delicacy: "Miss Churchill lost her seat, screamed and fell from her horse. A fall at such speed must have been violent; and yet it proved entirely to her advantage, for, without

being hurt, she gave the lie to all the unfavourable ideas that had been formed of her figure in judging from her face. The Duke alighted to help her. She was so stunned that her thoughts were far from occupied with questions of decency; and those who first crowded around her found her in a rather negligent posture. They could hardly believe that limbs of such exquisite beauty could belong to a face like Miss Churchill's."

But women did not lack underclothes. When the farthingale disappeared they used three petticoats, one over the other, to hold out their dresses, called "the modest one", "the mischievous one" and "the secret one". The *basquine* became a corset again. This new corset moulded the bust quite cruelly, but without giving it the stiff appearance of the Renaissance; women's bosoms were rounded again. It was now called a *gourgandine*. Transparent clothes came back. The seventeenth century taste for clothes is shown in the bawdy nicknames they were given then, like "musketeer", "innocent", "tumble", "wasps", "teaser", "touch here", "tempters", "saucy", "squeaky". The latter was the name given to a crackly material often used to make the bustles, pads and rolls that gave a look reminiscent of the farthingale.

The first publicity slogan for underwear appeared in the window of a corset-maker, advertising the felicitous effects of her latest model on the breasts: "it controls the large, sup-

Panniers and hoops, market 1719. The pannier probably derived from the *criardes*, underskirts made of a stiffened, crackly cloth. In 1718 this evolved into an horizontal garment ribbed with whalebone, somewhat rounded by 1725, and oval-shaped between 1725 and 1730. It then developed into a multiplicity of shapes, including the famous "elbow" pannier which provided armrests at the hipline. In 1730 the front section began to incline and by 1750 it had split into a double pannier which could be lifted up under the arms, thus solving the problem of its basic cumbersomeness. Right: Whalebone bodice in white satin decorated with coloured braid, circa 1660.

ports the small, uplifts the drooping". In fact since the Middle Ages the corset (or whatever name it was given according to the period) changed very little, and Montaigne's description was valid for a long time: "the corset is a sort of girdle that encases the body from beneath the breasts to the bottom of the ribs,

the need to be pinched, strangled, and squeezed in either round the hips or under the breasts, and from the Athenians' bands to the present day girdle, they have almost always been able to satisfy this inclination.

The moralists did, however, launch an attack against a new phenomenon: the speed of changes in

finishing in a point over the stomach". In the seventeenth century any variations were only details: sometimes it was stiff, other times more pliable; sometimes it laced in front, other times behind. Tired of condemning it on moral grounds or for reasons of hygiene, priests and doctors allowed it to take its course. It seems that in every age women feel

fashion. During the Renaissance, when breaking away from the styles perpetuated by tradition, people had already realised that dress was no longer something absolute, but was linked to a particular period. But in the late seventeenth century and early eighteenth century changes, even if they were slight, already took place so quickly that if someone was away from Paris for three months people laughed at their appearance when they returned. Priests threatened women who paid too much attention to elegance with fire and brimstone: "What can these unfortunate creatures expect but unheard-of disasters and rigorous punishment by God both in this world and the next."

In the eighteenth century people became aware of the relativity of fashion, and of the fact that its interest does not lie in any advantage afforded by change, but in change for its own sake. They also discovered that fashion cannot change without going back to styles that are out-of-date and long abandoned; in other words fashion moves in cycles.

Another eighteenth-century phe-

nomenon was that in the towns fashion imposed itself on all strata of society at the same time. When panniers appeared, cumbersome as they were, they were immediately adopted by the servant girls and the market women. A pannier was a hooped framework, made of circles of wicker, cord and whale-bone that fitted round the waist. More rounded and less extreme than the farthingale, the pannier nevertheless fulfilled the same function.

They had scarcely appeared when they provoked the protests of the same moralists who had earlier attacked the farthingale. The fashionable ladies were accused of wanting "to live and die in impenitence under the weight of their tiring and scandalous panniers" and "this seductive lure could incite the poor men to sin". But they were also greeted with comment from the men:

> Make your petticoat short that a hoop
> eight yards wide
> May decently shew how your garters
> are tied.

Poets were aware of the attraction of wide panniers that hid the legs:

> At times to veil is to reveal,
> And to display is to conceal;
> Mysterious are your laws!
> The vision's finer than the view;
> Her landscape Nature never drew
> So fair as fancy draws.

It is true that the pannier held the dress away from the body, making it more exciting and more accessible.

The series of revealing falls continued, from Sophie Arnould's fall

Busks of the 17th century. The busk, of a strip of bone, wood or metal passed down the middle of the front of a piquéd bodice ensured its rigidity. Carved or painted, made of ivory or damasked steel, even at times concealing a dagger, the busk was moveable: women could take it out to flirt with a gallant or to breathe more easily. The more pliant whalebone allowed the number of strips to be increased and led, towards the late 17th century, to the disappearance of the central busk.
Left: *Dressmaker Delivering Her Panniers*, by Dupin, after Le Clerc, Galerie des Modes, 1778.

from her donkey, to Mlle Lambercier's accident in front of the King of Sardinia, which moved Jean-Jacques Rousseau to declare: "I could not laugh about an accident, that, although funny in itself, made me concerned for a person I love like a mother, and perhaps more."

Paintings, drawings and engravings portray woman as a creature no longer protected by her clothes, at the mercy of a wandering hand or a gust of wind. Casanova was delighted that women's dress was so designed that it took only a second to disturb it, a second to put it back in place — a positive advantage at a time when people readily made love on a doorstep. Ladies in panniers obligingly perched on swings and were sketched by artists who did not tire of drawing their knees and garters and the lower parts of their thighs. But some

showed concern for modesty; an account in *The Spectator* of 1712 declares: "In this diversion there are very many pretty shrieks, not so much for fear of falling off as that their petticoats should untie. The lover who swings his lady is to tie her clothes very close together with his hat band before she admits him to throw up her heels."

After the compromise of the Renaissance, the segregation of clothing started in the Middle Ages was completed by the time these titillating engravings were produced. Although men still wore some ribbons and lace trimmings, the main distinctions were fixed; a fastened and closed costume for men, an open and often wide open one for women. The great paradox of western dress, that wants men to be protected by their dress from attacks they have no need to

fear, and women to be betrayed by theirs to mishaps they are far more likely to encounter, from this time on becomes a rule of nature soon to be made into a law which forbids women to wear male costume.

Under Louis XIV, men were still tempted to come closer to feminine clothes by adopting "petticoat-breeches", a long petticoat which was one of western man's last attempts to revert to flowing clothes. Although the petticoat-breeches disappeared, men were still very fond of bright colours, cascades of ribbons, billowing lace and rows and rows of flounces which they only started to give up just before the French Revolution, to adhere to the tenet that sober clothes are a sign of virility.

The Ribbon Seller Jeaurat, 18th century. <u>Below</u>: Whalebone bodice, French style, 1750. During this period the "body" was laced back and/or front, with shoulderstraps or even sleeves. It no longer concealed the breasts as it had done during the previous century, and stopped at the hips which were freed by slashed basks — the front pieces ending in a point. The amount of bone set into it meant it could weigh up to 700 grams. The backing was made of a relatively rough unbleached cloth, but the right side was of elegant, luxury fabrics.

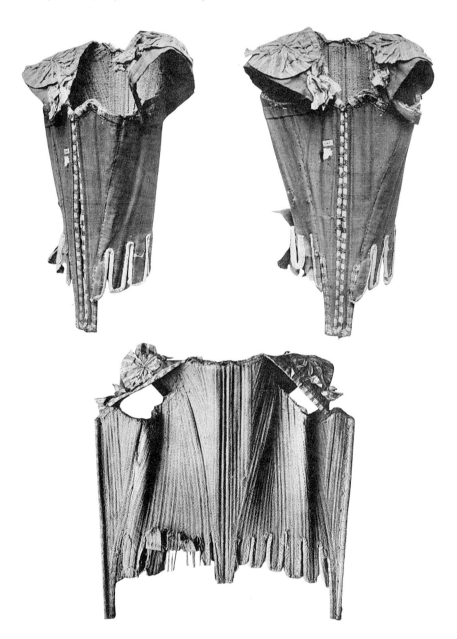

THE DISAPPEARANCE
OF THE CORSET

*I*t was not the Revolution that banished panniers and threw women's dresses into uncertainty. Confusion preceded rather than followed it.

The pannier disappeared towards the end of Louis XIV's reign, and in the years leading up to the fall of the Bastille clothes reflected the troubles of the time. Women did not know which school of fashion to follow. They hesitated between the ostentatious fashion led by Marie-Antoinette — until the *Affaire du Collier* and the advice of the philo-

sophers who counselled naturalness and simplicity. The ladies of the court who played at being shepherdesses at the Trianon with their elaborately coiffed hair and wigs, exemplified the contradiction of their lives in the last fifteen years before the Revolution. The corset was attacked by exponents of the healthy outdoor life, and a pamphlet appeared in 1773 entitled "The degradation of the human race through the wearing of whalebone corsets". Through the didactic philosophy of

*C*uirasses to prevent stabbings — caricature, around 1815. For a few years, there was a rumour in Paris that maniacs were enjoying themselves stabbing ladies' bottoms.
<u>Left</u>: Galleries of the Palais Royal, detail, Boilly, circa 1800.

"Polish style" dress, France, 1780. This style reveals the new liking for more athletic figures. The loop skirt is no longer fashionable, hips are getting thinner, the bulge goes to the back in the shape of a small "pouf". For the "Polish-style" dress, the pouf consists of three folds tucked up by drawstring braids — The whole thing is supported by a cushion stuffed with horsehair called the *cul* that is all the rage until Revolution. At the same time the archaic funnel-shaped garment stiffened with whalebone gives way to an "English-style" corset the seams of which follow the curves of the waist.
<u>Below</u>: *Dressing.* Lavreince, end of the 18th century.

Jean-Jacques Rousseau it became fashionable to expect ladies to breast-feed their babies themselves, and to wear the kind of practical clothes that would allow them to walk in the fields. The corset resisted, but the pannier succumbed, and gave rise to the bustle (this time called a *cul*) as the farthingale had done.

The bustle gave women much more freedom of movement and they liked it, because unlike the pannier which gave them an unnatural profile, the bustle, a deceptive garment, enhanced their natural shape. These horse-hair pads, fastened to the small of the back, became popular almost overnight so a lady who had been away from Paris for just a few months, returned to find her clothes completely out-of-date.

In physical appearance women in the reign of Louis XVI resembled

those of the time of Louis XV: plump, dimpled, with rounded, promising thighs. The female attributes — breasts and bottom — were displayed to advantage. The disappearance of the pannier allowed women to play at copying men's clothes; with dresses like frock-coats, waistcoats, flat-heeled shoes and a cane in their hands. They were not trying to adopt men's clothes seriously, as they had done in the Renaissance; they only borrowed some details from their costume and used them in a flirtatious and provocative way. In the twentieth century the same thing happens again, but once more without jeopardizing the fundamental ideas of different styles of dress for the two sexes.

Women enjoyed handling their canes with an air of bravado, playing at being chemists or agricultural ex-

perts, debating the constitution with all the seriousness of social reformers. They gained a freedom of behaviour which they used to advantage like an additional charm. But since the structure of their costume had not changed, they could not adopt the stance of a young man without risking mishaps. Thiébault relates how a crowd gathered beneath a window in the rue du Faubourg-Saint-Honoré because a lady was sitting reading with her feet up on the edge of the balcony, unwittingly affording a disturbing sight to passers-by. But women still did not think of resorting to drawers, and not even the hazards of life during the Revolution could persuade them to alter their ways.

The Revolution contributed nothing original to women's dress, which continued along the lines it had adopted at the beginning of Louis XVI's reign. In furniture, the camber had disappeared at the same time as the pannier, and during the revolutionary period the straightness of line was simply accentuated. The corset, which had been getting smaller, disappeared, and was replaced like the pannier, by pads worn on the hips. Without the corset the breasts were supported by a neckerchief which was first tied at the throat, and then under the chin where it was eventually reinforced with extra stiffening. Like the bustle it was a deceptive garment designed to emphasize natural features.

The young women on their way to the guillotine, and those who watched them, wore only a chemise and a petticoat beneath their simple straight dresses. Their underwear had the simplicity of ancient Greece or the Merovingian period.

D*ressing* —
Lavreince, end of the 18th century.
<u>Left</u>: On the eve of the Revolution, women's clothes tend to be more and more standardized due to the egalitarian simplicity of the "English-style" fashions and to the growing liking for the simple world of servants, linen maids and female workers. The underwear is very simple, without hoop skirts or stiffeners; it consists mainly of a small corset worn over a light shirt, a petticoat and paddings on the hips. Most women now wear those simple underclothes whatever their class.

The Directory may have been a counter-revolution because it made rich materials fashionable again, but in other things it followed a course that had already begun. Parisian women very deliberately matched their clothes to the ideas of the times, in which the Greeks and the Romans cropped up in every discussion. They called their dresses tunics: they were long and straight and had slashed skirts and they resembled the chiton much more than any of the dresses, all to some extent padded out and drawn in, that had been worn since the fifteenth century. The only kind of corset worn under these tunics was a zona; bands were wrapped around the body as the Greek women had done, except that now they were worn slightly higher and supported the lower part of the chest. The passion for transparent tunics and even close-fitting underwear made the young women strolling in the Champs Elysées look like nymphs surprised at their toilet. The trend towards modesty and simplicity in clothes that started under Rousseau's influence, had reached its end and turned elegant women into courtesans. When a fashion has become as extreme as this, there is nothing to do but turn back. Shoulder straps were added to the zona and it became a corset again. This time it was less cruel; it had elastic instead of whalebones, and was covered with satin or velvet.

At the end of the Consulate and the beginning of the Empire an aristocracy, a mixture of the old and the new, formed again, and on Napoleon's own orders dressed themselves up in luxurious clothes with a clear conscience. The sumptuousness of the first receptions of the imperial regime equalled that of the old order. Ribbons, muslins, cascades of velvet and satin, billows of crepe flowed under the re-gilded ceilings. Hidden by the dress, corsets were again boned and went down to the waist where small rolls were attached to them to enhance women's rounded contours. The ultra-fashionable women of the Directory had been tall, thin and straight; under the Empire they were to be plump and buxom, wholesome and fecund.

Although the style of the Empire was more opulent, it still preserved the line of the Directory style and dresses were not so very different from the tunics. They differed because they were made of thicker materials and the waist was high under the breasts, but from there they fell straight, barely flaring out, and were still reminiscent of Greek clothes. Under the corset women wore only a chemise, nothing covered the lower part of the body. Women were decent because no

Parisian Fashion, by Vernet, circa 1800. Below: *Outraged Modesty*, or *The Disadvantage of Veils*, Directory period; *Indispensable New Year Gifts*, caricature of wigs, around 1816.

Elastic corset, French model, 1804; X-shaped linen corset, French model, 1810.
Below: Corset maker, Gratine after Lante, 1820.
Right: *Morning*, Numa Bassaget, 1830 (above left); *It is exactly the size of Venus*, Octave Tassaert, 1830 (above right); *The corset seller*, Numa Bassaget, 1830 (below left); *I can't believe it ..... 4 sizes bigger*, Honore Daumier, 1840 (below right).

panniers or bustles held their skirts out, and yet they could easily be hitched up, which is just what the Emperor intended.

The tyranny of the corset towards the bust increased as society became more stable at the end of the Empire and during the Restoration. The fashion was for the breasts to be far apart, and this could only be achieved with a rather evil bone structure invented by the corset-maker Leroy. The corset disappeared in the Revolution along with the aristocrats, returned with the émigrés at the beginning of the Empire, and came into its own under Louis XVIII. The sexes were poles apart in the society he inherited from Napoleon. Woman's role was to beguile her soldier's leisure, bear his children and be a good cook. Under the new regime women obtained no further rights, and a young girl's innocence was a guarantee of her virtue, but since she was no longer required to have lots of pregnancies to make up for the losses on the battlefield she was allowed to have her waist strangled and her stomach crushed by a corset. Charles X did not approve of this fashion: "It used to be quite common to find Dianas, Venuses and Niobes in France, but now there are only wasps."

This comment reflects the changes in fashion over half a century. With the disappearance of the pannier and the bustle there was a movement towards straight dresses like the Greeks wore, "à la Diane" as Charles X said, when he ordered the progressive abolition of underwear. A movement in the opposite direction had crept in at the beginning of the Empire. It triumphed under the Restoration, and the accentuated waist and flared skirt were back, although skirts were not yet held out by a pannier but by layers of petticoats. Women returned to wider hips at the same moment that furniture, which had been all straight lines since Louis XVI, rediscovered curves. Both women and furniture were nostalgic for the Louis XV style. In a few more years, the pannier was to reappear under the name of crinoline. The crinoline fastened on to the sides of a corset that was even more cruel than that of the eighteenth century; the breasts were encased in cups and it also covered the thighs and became a suspender belt for the first time. Over all this armour trousers ballooned out — yet another revival of past fashion.

B E D , B E A C H
A N D B O A R D S

1. Nightwear

Women started wearing the nightgown again in the six-teenth century, after centuries of sleeping in the nude. In remote country areas the old fashion persisted longer, but otherwise the adoption of the nightshirt was universal, and had only one exception — the wedding night.

Some historians maintain the opposite, citing something Cathos says in *Les Précieuses Ridicules:* "All I can say, uncle, is that I find marriage altogether shocking. How can one bear to think about sleeping next to a man who is completely naked?" Cathos has just arrived from the provinces, and by putting a peasant-girl's words into the mouth of a girl eager to learn the ways of Paris, Molière intended to amuse his audience. Or perhaps he was alluding to the conventions of the wedding night that still existed in the provinces. Also Cathos is very young and naive, and was perhaps a new experience for

Valery Taylor, *Ballet Today*, April 1954. Bathing costume, Diana-Slip, France, 1931. Photo: Schall

the audience. In addition, it is not impossible that out of modesty, Cathos used the word "sleep" for "to make love". Recent research has indicated that in puritan countries, notably the United States, propriety required that nightclothes should be kept on to make love, but this was not the case in the seventeenth and eighteenth centuries, when people hardly ever hestitated to disrobe.

Nightgowns were worn until quite late in the day, and in the seventeenth century it was quite normal for ladies to receive visitors while still in bed. Or they would sometimes lie on the covers wearing a transparent robe over their nightgown. It was not considered at all shocking to receive a visitor in this state, even a stranger. The bedroom did not become sacrosanct until the nineteenth century.

Before then people spent a lot of time lounging in the bedroom rather as they do today on a beach. Although modesty had made some progress in the streets, it was barely noticeable inside a house. It did not exist at all between women. A fashionable Parisian lady was washed, dressed and had her hair done by her maids, and might have some of her friends there as onlookers, or even an unknown lady who happened to call while she was dressing. The apothecary and his assistants could come and go at this time too. A valet might enter the room as she was dressing without anyone bothering, and if a male visitor arrived, the lady would be prettily confused. Yet there were signs that modesty was gaining ground under the influence of the Reformation and the Counter-Reformation; for example Louis XIV issued a decree authorizing women who hitherto had only been sewing-maids to do the same work as tailors so that ladies' modesty would be safeguarded during fittings.

In the eighteenth century nightgowns became more complicated and were fastened with laces to emphasize the waist and free the shoulders. This garment was called *casaquin* and looked like a corset with a petticoat attached at the waist and falling to the knees. It took the place of the nightgown and was popular with ladies and servants alike. Artists were of course delighted with this garment that left the breasts and the legs uncovered. Quite often in summer

women slept naked and put on a *casaquin* to receive visitors.

This kind of behaviour which encouraged licentiousness, contrasts with that of the nineteenth century when only a courtesan would receive someone in her bedroom. Like the other underclothes of the period the nightgown became a suit of armour; it was starched, laced and buttoned and enveloped the woman from the neck to the wrists and ankles. Men remained faithful to the nightshirt until 1900 when they adopted pyjamas, thus completing the masculinization of their clothes that had started back in the Middle Ages.

In keeping with their growing emancipation from 1914 to 1926, women changed their nightclothes radically. Nightgowns were shorter, and instead of the stiff cloths required by the nineteenth-century propriety, they were made of lighter, often transparent materials.

At the same time women watched the evolution of men's pyjamas. It was logical that men should exchange their open nighshirts for close-fitting pyjamas. Since the Middle Ages they had been concentrating on distinguishing their clothes from women's. They were men and they wanted that fact to be obvious.

Initially the desire for different costume was erotic, but this disappeared and by the nineteenth century it was simply a question of respectability. The staid nineteenth century got rid of whatever remained

common to the dress of both sexes, even small details. The last ribbons were removed and the last coloured clothes for men were replaced by dark ones, the last embroideries were relegated to the uniforms of the Academicians. The nightshirt, the final vestige of Antiquity, offended men's dignity by forcing them to wear open clothes at night when for centuries such clothes had symbolized femininity. Pyjamas did away with this last ambiguity.

But women had been playing at imitating men for a long time. This did not disturb the men because the women did not encroach on their territory, on the contrary they made it clear they were only copying men for fun. They adopted pyjamas and turned them into frivolous garments so that there was no question of unsurping masculinity.

Pyjamas allowed a lot of freedom of

action and with a dressing gown over the top a town-dweller could easily slip out to buy fresh bread for breakfast. This led to the development of the wide beach pyjamas which were the forerunners of other kinds of summer trousers.

After World War II the nightdress gained on pyjamas, just as the slip did on cami-knickers. A lot of women wore only the pyjama jacket and so manufacturers started making short nightdresses to the tops of the thighs. Since contemporary fashion in underwear demands many differing and contrasting styles they made long trimmed, beribboned, see-through nightdresses too. The speed with which fashions change nowadays, coupled with the large demand and the limited number of styles available led to short nightdresses that had drawers or panties — a return to light, transparent and startlingly feminine pyjamas.

The only enemy for nightwear to fight now is nudity. Since the beginning of the century the hygiene-conscious northerners have been saying that the only way to sleep properly is to sleep without clothes. Among the lower classes where underwear is a sign of social advance, the nightdress is unassailable, but fashionable women may freely boast of sleeping in the nude. The German and Scandinavian health experts have undoubtedly played their part in spreading the fashion for sleeping naked, but sensuality is also an important factor. No one will deny that sleeping in the nude is pleasurable and it affords a particular kind of pleasure, for its erotic qualities act on oneself as well as the partner.

The same applies to bathing costumes. In the twentieth century everything changes radically from the nineteenth; women can be almost naked when bathing, but their motivation is very different from that of the Greeks.

2. Bathing Costumes

The habit of bathing in a chemise that women had adopted in the Middle Ages remained until the seventeenth and eighteenth centuries. But bathing itself was no longer very fashionable. One cannot imagine Louis XIV following Charlemagne's example and diving in naked with his courtiers, nor would the idea of building thermal baths have occurred to him. The lakes of Versailles were only intended to reflect the brightness of the sun, the stars and the fireworks, and to carry sumptuous gondolas in which the court would lie to listen to music. Bathing in the sea was considered therapeutic; bathing in the river was something the peasants did.

The aristocracy started to imitate them early in the eighteenth century with a sensuality that is illustrated in Watteau's paintings and evident in the bathing of Casanova's young mistresses. During the course of the century the English interest in sport,

Nightdress. Cadolle, France, 1943; silk and inserted lace. Lace modesty with large front bow.

the passion for nature introduced by the pre-romantics, the desire to imitate rustic behaviour that led the ladies of the court to play at being shepherdesses, combined to turn bathing into a pleasurable pastime, if not an institution. People bathed in the rivers as they had done in the Middle Ages: the men naked, the women in chemises.

Shortly before the Revolution bathing became an agreeable exercise for the Parisian gentry just as it had been for the Greeks and Romans. People started to swim again. Swimming schools were opened on the Seine, the most elegant one at the end of the Ile-Saint-Louis. It was an enormous swimming pool where nudity was not permitted; men wore drawers. The first strokes were tried out at the end of a rope held by the instructor. Only custom prevented women from going there. Between 1780 and 1790 only four or five had the courage to try it, and Thiébault, the future general, who was a regular client, as were the future Louis-Philippe and his two brothers, remarked on what he considered the foolhardiness of a man who brought his wife to bathe with these young men who were almost naked. This intrepid lady wore a costume she had designed herself, consisting of close fitting trousers and a pleated chemisette which revealed nothing but her head and her hands. She had scarcely got into the water when all the young men jumped in on the

pretext of holding her up; no part of her body escaped their attentions, and "borne up like Venus from the waves" the poor girl had no alternative but to leave the water and go and hide her confusion in a cabin. This incident shows that at the end of the eighteenth century a woman could not go swimming with men without them considering it the occasion for an orgy. Men continued to go swimming and by the end of the Empire they were bathing naked in the Seine outside the swimming pools. During the Restoration the police put a stop to this practice in large towns.

Anglomania led French women to sea-bathing for which they wore a dress whereas the English wore a dress and wide billowing trousers. They only left their cabins after a bell

Japanese women in bathing costumes, circa 1900.
Below: Bathing costumes, circa 1920. The evolution of the bathing costume made rapid advances when the one-piece knitted swimsuit appeared in the 1920s, leaving the arms and legs bare.
Left: Bather, England, 1894. The bathing costume shrank towards the end of the 19th century, but modesty required the use of a large wrap which one removed for bathing and put on again as soon as one came out of the water. At the same time, some magazines advised wearing, for aesthetic reasons, a rubber corset underneath the costume.

Bathers, Deauville, 1925.
<u>Below</u>: Arrest of a young sportswoman on a Chicago beach in 1922. Her costume offended Al Capone's fellow citizens.

had rung ordering the men to leave the beach. They went down to the sea wearing a bathing-robe, they bathed, held up by female attendants who then wrapped their robes round them again, led them back to their cabins, rubbed them dry and dressed them again. They fled at the sound of another bell which announced that the men were coming back to bathe. Any woman with a pair of field-glasses laid herself open to slander because men still bathed in the nude. A notion dating from ancient Rome still existed in England at the beginning of Queen Victoria's reign: modesty was a woman's duty and so she had to bathe in clothes and turn her head away when men, who had no modesty to observe, appeared on the beach in the nude.

In southern Europe the summer heat made bathing a necessity as well as an agreeable pastime, so the au-

sterity of the Counter-Reformation was resisted more strongly than elsewhere, and in the first part of the nineteenth century it was not dominated by English puritanism. Nevertheless men and women bathed separately, as in the north. Mérimée shows his talent as an accurate reporter as well as a good novelist when describing the women bathing in the Guadalquivir in the middle of Cordoba in *Carmen*.

"The moment the angelus rings it is considered to be night. At the last sound of the bell the women undress and take to the water. There are shouts and laughter, an unholy din." On this occasion darkness replaces the bathing costume, but not perfectly and "the men study the bathers from the embankments".

The bathing costume did not become common for men until the second half of the nineteenth century. And still in the countryside and the small French towns men bathed naked later than this.

Between 1900 and 1940 women's

bathing costumes followed the same trend as underwear and got smaller and smaller. At first they wore a short dress with trousers that fitted tightly at the knee, then the two garments were combined to become one which each year was a little shorter and a little less baggy that the last. By the time the 1914 war broke out arms, shoulders and half of the thighs were visible. The cloth moulded the breasts and the buttocks suggestively. During the war the tops of the legs became almost completely bare, the neckline was cut lower and there was even a cut in the sides, fastened by a lace, which boldly revealed the body down to the hip.

By now the function of the bathing costume is to mould the parts of the body that still have to be covered. The sun-bathing cult allows a woman lying on her stomach to pull her costume down to the small of the back. Little girls start to wear two-piece costumes and are closely followed by adults. Finally people are permitted to change publicly without the shelter of a cabin or tent; modesty stops where the beach starts and if in the course of getting dressed again a woman's briefs are seen it does not matter at all because they do not reveal any more than a bathing costume.

Nowadays there are numerous types of bathing costume (just as there are of underclothes). A woman might wear a bikini, which appeared about 1950 (and is identical with the one the Roman women wore), a one-piece costume in the style of 1930, perhaps with her legs covered to mid-thighs in the style of 1913. She might even go so far as to wear a

monokini, a pair of briefs with perfectly useless straps destined to disappear as soon as permission to bare the breasts is confirmed, which might happen since, in spite of frequent changes in style and some hostile reactions, it is quite clear that for more than fifty years the tendency is for bathers to wear less and less.

For the rest, many young women have bathed or sun-bathed nude either in a secluded cove or on one of the beaches of the Riviera where nudity is customary. Midnight swims and boating provide other opportunities for stripping. At a trial in Cannes

Eva Paneth on a beach, circa 1930. Photo Fritz Paneth.
Below: Beach pyjamas, Switzerland, circa 1930.

French swimsuits, in the 1930s.
Below: Two-piece bathing costume, from Gétien, 1947. Artificial fibres, more particularly nylon, developed by America during the war years, brought about a revolution in swimwear manufacturing, improving comfort and shape. Very soon the two-piece was reduced to the "bikini" — a name invented by Réard's and inspired by the Pacific atoll where the Americans had been carrying out nuclear tests.

a few years ago of an offence against modesty, it was stated plainly that it was only an offence because it was done with commercial intent — which is one way of saying that provided it is not done for mercenary reasons, nudity on a beach is not a crime. Most of the nudists who are fanatical about the natural life are German or Scandinavian, some idolize the sun, but many of them are sensualists who like to feel air and water on all parts of their bodies. Of the latter a large number derived additional pleasure from knowing that they are breaking a law. Men tattooed and painted themselves all the colours of the rainbow; they wore masks and feathers to break free from nature, and one can take off one's clothes in the open air to free oneself from society.

The sense of physical well-being experience by a woman who bathed without clothes in fifth century Athens, bears no relation to the feelings of the young woman ostensibly imitating her on the beaches around St. Tropez. The modern young woman knows that her nudity is somewhat irregular and subversive. A girl who decides not to put on her briefs on a warm summer day is constantly and sensuously aware of not wearing them, whereas a seventeenth-century woman who never wore them never missed them; a woman who leaves off a nightdress feels a positive physical pleasure unlike her predecessor in the thirteenth century for whom it was quite normal to sleep naked; the girl who exposes her body to the waves and the wind and also to men's eyes, has a different experience from the Cretan woman — and it can be even more disturbing for her if she was brought up in a convent where the Victorian influence until a few years ago still required the pupils to wear a chemise to take a shower (although in the reign of Louis XIV a woman undressed completely to wash).

It would be a mistake to assume that the only likely outcome in the evolution of women's bathing costumes is nudity. What will characterize women in the second half of the twentieth century is that they will sometimes swim and sunbathe without any clothes, and at others will wear a bathing costume in any of the styles that have existed since ancient times — and moreover they will use materials and styles that have hitherto been used only for underwear (in the United States they have already started to do this). They will be more and more inclined to mix bedroom and beach wear and use net, lace and

transparent materials — in short make beachwear what it was at the time a chemise was worn: an undergarment that can be shown openly in front of other people on the beach.

3. Dance Costumes

Under the name of subligaculum drawers were obligatory for dancers in Rome. When they disappeared in the seventeenth century the dancer's freedom of movement in front of an audience was limited. It is quite certain that if any women in Europe needed drawers it was the dancers. In the eighteenth century when their art became more precise they still could not move freely, or out of modesty had to hide their legs under a long dress and so they suffered from

being compared unfavourably with their male partners who could freely exhibit all their talents.

It was only under Louis XV when Mlle Mariette had the misfortune to get her skirt caught up on a piece of scenery, and got more applause for her anatomy than her art that the policy ordered all dancers to wear drawers. The same law also applied to actresses because the spectacle they afforded might disturb the prompters.

But the actresses who were not particularly concerned about the prompters' peace of mind, and had nothing to gain from wearing this strange garment, resisted the obligation to wear it quite fiercely, and it was difficult for the police to determine whether or not they were doing so. Casanova was vexed by this question and often asked actress friends who usually replied they did not. It is interesting to note in passing that he called these drawers *culottes* — thus anticipating vocabulary by more than a century.

On the other hand many dancers like la Camargo, took to wearing drawers enthusiastically because with their protection, they felt they had the right to shorten their skirts. So in 1775 they created a fashion which was not to become women's everyday wear until after 1925, and the audience could see the way they executed every movement. Nevertheless this new trend provoked some uneasiness among audiences; Grimm says: "The Jansenists cried heresy and scandal and did not approve of short skirts. The Jesuits on the other hand, claimed that this innovation brought us closer to the primitive Church which did not want to see pirouettes and *gargouillades* executed badly because of the petticoats. The council of the Opéra had a lot of trouble establishing a sound doctrine on this point of discipline which divided the faithful."

Men were at first confused, but after a period of reflection they decided short skirts were a good thing, and no longer disliked drawers for covering up women's legs; in fact they decided they rather approved of them because they "made what they

hid even more desirable." If you remember that the Renaissance drawers were completely forgotten by this time, and that this garment that dancers were obliged to wear was not worn by any other women, then it is not surprising that men hesitated and wondered whether this new article, enforced by the authorities in the name of morality, was not rather perverse. There was nothing about the underwear of the period to prepare them for the modern erotic process which rests on balancing opposites and requires something to be offered and forbidden at the same time. And this was what drawers did; they allowed the most daring movements to be seen, but not in detail, they covered the buttocks but outlined their shape. An article in a newspaper published in 1779 notes that: "Drawers permit the dancers to execute the splits, do turns and pirouettes on one foot and the fact that they hide their legs only excites the audience even more." A new dimension in sensibility had been discovered.

Drawers soon started to be made out of a thin, supple flesh-coloured material, like that used later by the women of the Directory, and they spread to dancers all over Europe as skirts and petticoats continued to get shorter. This was only stopped by the middle-class modesty of the Restora-

nature of their art and knew that the public appreciated both the grace of a figure and the skill of a step.

The classical dancers did not take their opposition as far as Lola Montès who, relying on the scandal rather then her talent, appeared on the stage in the early part of ·Louis-

The Moulin Rouge ball, circa 1900. Below: Anna Pavlova, circa 1910.

tion. As administrator of the Opéra, Sosthène de la Rochefoucauld tried to ban the close-fitting drawers and decided to substitute wide baggy trousers like those worn by little girls, to hide the figure. But uniforms, whether military, ecclesiastical or artistic, are much less susceptible to change than ordinary clothes. The dancers were set on keeping their close-fitting tights, and they resisted the change all the more fiercely because for centuries they had been accustomed to anticipating fashion rather than copying that of children. They were aware of the ambiguous

Philippe's reign, without drawers or trousers. But they fiercely defended their right to wear tights, and eventually this right was no longer questioned. The charms that Sosthène de la Rochefoucauld had considered incompatible with the seriousness of the dance, assumed such importance in the second half of the nineteenth century that everything conspired to enhance the voluptuousness of the dancer's thighs and bottom. Petticoats were made much shorter until they became "tutus", longer than those worn today, but above the knee. The bottom petticoat was sewn

between the legs to avoid accidents,
because the seam of the tights might
split and reveal the dancer's most
intimate charms to the curious public. But this was not the only reason.
Prudence was allied with eroticism.
Delicate muslins were used to cover
the dancer's hips and thighs. These
flimsy materials were not intended to
envelop the figure demurely as Sosthène de la Rochefoucauld wished, but
to cloak it without hiding it. Too
much prudery would have been out of
place at this time because people
went to the theatre or ballet to
release their emotions, since in their
everyday clothes women were enclosed in extravagant corsets and
crinolines. The low-class dance-halls
where they danced the can-can, the
music-halls which showed *couchers*,

and after 1905, strip shows, would
have proved too much competition
for classical dance if the latter had
not consented to join in with the
attractions that the times made
necessary. The Opéra had the sense
to offer excitement to the rich
middle-class Parisians, to provide
subjects for artists, and to inspire the
genius of Degas because the only bare
legs to be seen at the end of the
nineteenth century were in the dressing rooms or on the stage.

The short skirt that used to be
worn over the tutu disappeared and
the top petticoat took its place. It is
rare for an under-garment to become
an outer one, although the reverse
happens more frequently: for example the chemise was an outer tunic
that had become an under-garment.
In sports clothes one finds changes
comparable to the evolution of the
tutu — for example bloomers became
outer clothes in the twentieth century — although the reasons behind
the changes in sports clothes are
different. The dancer feels the need
for fewer and lighter clothes, like the
sportswoman, but does not necessari-
ly choose what is practical, and
having to choose between the tutu
and the skirt, opts for flimsy gauze —
because she is more concerned to
wear something that will set off her
movements than with rational
changes in dress.

At present the fashion in dancers'
costumes obeys two rules — lightness
and moderation. The petticoat that

was joined between the legs has disappeared, and dancers wear a leotard or tights. They sometimes leave off their tutus, but it would be hasty to assume that dance costumes may eventually be only leotards and tights. If the tutu were to disappear it would soon be restored by a resurgence of femininity. In the event that at some time in the future, dance finds a place for the short tunic, this will go very well with tights, and the latter are already so successful that they were adopted first for winter sports and now for everyday wear.

Tights started to be worn in the mountains under ski-pants and then under trousers and dresses worn in town. They were made of different textures and colours, and from them developed the body-stocking or cat-suit that fits tightly from the shoulders to the feet, often made of the kind of lace which looks good on the legs as well as the body. This vogue came from America. It is a totally impractical garment and seems intended only to be put on under a dress that is shortly to be taken off. It is typical of the intriguing underwear that is prevalent today.

So, thanks to dancers, Renaissance drawers reappeared at the end of the eighteenth century, and survived during the first part of the nineteenth when women's thighs were normally bare under their skirts. They were fined down to give that impression of clothed nudity on the stage which could excite a whole audience.

Ballerina, 1950s. Tutu, back view. Photo E. Boubat.

DRAWERS AND PANTALOONS

The seventeenth and eighteenth centuries managed quite well without drawers. They persisted in the wardrobes of a few horse-women but many amusing tales of falls show that quite often women didn't bother to put them on. In Louis XV's reign, a decree made them obligatory for dancers. They showed this new garment off quite happily, but even if it stirred the men's imagination, it was not a success with the women of Paris, a few courtesans excepted. One would have thought that the women who dressed themselves up to look like boys just before the Revolution would have taken to drawers to protect their virtue; this was not so.

Although some ladies at the courts of Czars and Swedish kings, in German and even in French high society, did wear men's clothes and travelled the country in a free-and-easy masculine way, such cases were rare and did not change the normal custom. At the end of the eighteenth century the future general Thiébault

Caricature of a woman dressed as a man. Louis-Philippe period. <u>Left</u>: Crinoline, circa 1860. The fashion designer Worth claimed that the Empress Eugénie had introduced the crinoline to conceal her pregnancy — the Prince Imperial was born in 1856. Queen Victoria, in a similar condition, was also thought to have adopted this timely fashion. But the crinoline had made its appearance as early as 1845.

met an elegantly dressed young horseman, who turned out to be a girl of good family travelling with her father. Thiébault, who took some time to realize it was not a man, remarked that the occurrence was unusual, but was not shocked by it, as a man would have been in the nineteenth or early twentieth century. Similarly, men sometimes wore women's clothes — for a fancy-dress ball or to go unnoticed to a lovers' rendezvous. Du Cause de Nazelle, who lived at the time of Louis XIV, relates in his *Mémoires* how he disguised himself as a maid or a laundress to go and visit his mistress. This trick seemed quite innocuous to him; nowadays it would be scandalous. In the seventeenth century the medieval project succeeded: differences in costume distinguished men from women, but it was still not dishonourable for a man to wear a dress.

The French women who wore men's clothes at the time of the Breton royalist uprising or in the Republican army to serve a cause or to follow a lover, were again the exception rather than the rule. Only at the end of the Revolution was a law passed forbidding women to wear men's clothes. This law, the first to codify the segregation of dress, was passed not because the Parisian women had been abusing trousers, but because of the prudish and conservative customs of the middle classes who had come to power.

Even the aristocratic ladies who fled through the countryside during the Reign of Terror rarely discarded their feminine clothes, and the fashion for patriotic spankings made only a small number of middle-class women sew up a few inches at the bottom of their chemises to make combinations. The spankings were administered in the street by Republican ruffians to women who looked too aristocratic. But this violence, which even alarmed German nuns who also sewed their chemises, did not last long, and the garment it had given rise to was forgotten straight away. The egalitarian zeal of the Republicans had earlier on scared some women into thinking they would have to wear trousers. On 29 October 1793 the Convention issued a proclamation to reassure all citizenesses that they would not be forced to wear trousers, that their open clothes in no way conflicted "with Republican morals".

The transparent, flesh-coloured underwear that some of the fashionable ladies wore under the Directory was not really a form of drawers; it was a ruse to appear naked without in fact being so. The name drawers, given to it by Mme Tallien, survived because Parisian men took it up again in 1807 when women started to appear at the Palais-Royal and on the Boulevards with lace frills round their ankles, suggesting that they were wearing a new under-garment. These frills were stitched to the bottom of long wide trousers made of fine linen

or lawn which tied round the waist and helped give fullness to the skirt.

These trousers — often called pantaloons or pantalettes — were not just suddenly invented. They had been worn for thirty years in Anglo-Saxon countries. For example, in Holland at the end of the eighteenth century skaters had started wearing the drawers worn by dancers, and servant girls copied the skaters when they had to climb a ladder or clean the windows, to stop the boys looking at them. Drawers were first introduced as a puritan offensive which suited a middle-class Protestant nation. In England girls wore drawers to do gymnastics, and little girls wore them to play. Women started to wear them for hunting, and even in town, in spite of the scandal they created.

Progressive spirits proclaimed the usefulness of trousers, several doctors recommended them. One of them claimed that "by stopping the passage of air, as a woman walks or dances, they prevent rheumatism and other discomforts". This defence went unheeded. At court only Queen Hortense wore trousers, and that was presumably to conform to Dutch morality. The Parisian bourgeoisie who associated them with dancers, thought them brazen, and they were not altogether wrong, because if the ladies intended only to protect their virtue and guard against rheumatism, they did not need to wear them so long that they showed beneath their dresses and attracted attention.

Under pressure of public opinion they had to give up trousers a few months after they started wearing them. They were not even allowed for riding. The *Journal des Dames* declared that a horsewoman's mod-

esty was assured by a wide coloured petticoat falling to the horse's hock and fastened to her foot by a small gold chain. Trousers could not be worn for fencing either, a long straight dress was sufficient, and if they wanted to imitate men the only thing they could wear was a Bradenburg. They had to do gymnastics to wear wide sailors' trousers under an enormous silk blouse.

Wearing trousers was very quickly limited to the young girls who did gymnastics and the prostitutes who had no intention of discarding trousers that fluttered round their legs and attracted men's attention. We have already seen that courtesans seized on any new underwear, and also that they went on wearing it long after it had become unfashionable, simply in order to be conspicuous. The fact that they went on wearing trousers would have made these garments a symbol of debauchery and prevented their being worn at all in the middle-class society of the nineteenth century if they had not also been worn by little girls. It was not the first time that dancers, courtesans and little girls wore the same garment: the same had occurred in ancient Rome. Nevertheless this was the first time for a long period that children's dress differed from general adults' wear.

The Middle Ages strove to distinguish between men and women with two uniforms, but the idea of distinguishing children from grown-ups had never arisen. Small girls and boys wore exactly the same clothes as adults from the day they were no longer in swaddling clothes. Childhood was not considered a separate world. The most indelicate jokes were told in front of small children, even in the best society. As soon as a boy could ride a horse it was normal for him to take part in a battle. At seven he learned foreign languages, at eleven his sister was married and made love quite legitimately.

The notes taken by Louis XIII's doctor prove that at the beginning of the seventeenth century it was still natural for a boy to be encouraged to masturbate, and his instructresses willingly accepted his first amorous overtures. At that time children of seven gambled and read the same books as adults. The only difference in clothes was that until the age of eight or nine boys were dressed like girls — a habit which persisted until World War I, except that in the last decade this travesty had ended at age four or five.

The origin of this peculiarity lies in the great medieval change in dress. Men had started wearing breeches and their gowns had become jackets or coats whilst women's clothes had remained the same. It seemed unnecessary to make little boys' clothes like men's whilst they were still in the women's hands. The women were conservative about things that concerned them, and this applied to the little boys they brought up. It was not that they wanted to dress them like girls, but that they kept them in their traditional clothes. When they reached the age of discretion the transition began and boys wore breeches under their dresses before relinquishing them altogether, or they wore breeches and dresses alternately. As a result of this the children in sixteenth, seventeenth and eighteenth-century paintings are difficult to judge: the prettier ones especially, the more dressed up they are the more they all look like charming young girls.

In a slow struggle which lasted right throughout the seventeenth and eighteenth centuries, many moralists spread the idea of children's innocence, succeeded in getting school books expurgated slightly, persuaded adults to modify their conversations for certain ears: in short, they invented childhood. By the end of the eighteenth century clothes had begun to feel the effect. In theory girls were still dressed like women, but increasingly they were allowed to leave off the pannier and then the corset until it became quite normal for their clothes to be made looser so they could play more easily. For the same reason boys at the time of Louis XVI were allowed to wear wide cloth trousers, fifty years before middle-class adults adopted them.

Girls went right on wearing lace-trimmed pantaloons after 1807 partly because they felt they resembled their

brothers' thicker ones. But their mothers did not copy them, because the moralists, aided by Jean-Jacques Rousseau, had achieved their aim, and it was accepted that childhood was a world apart — and had its own clothing. So trousers, considered indecent for women, were modesty itself for little girls. Only one or two particularly conservative families refused to dress their daughters in trousers, and told them instead to pay more attention to the way they moved.

Mlle de Condé, an émigré living in London, disapproved of trousers because they allowed children to exchange the dignity that used to be required of them for improper ex-

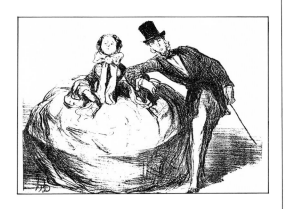

uberance: "Instead of the seemly behaviour and obligations of propriety of my childhood, I see girls in trousers running around and showing their legs above the knee, pushing each other, throwing each other on the ground, rolling on the grass." This criticism was directed less against trousers themselves than against the licence they gave little girls to play boisterous games. Mlle de Condé believed in the old medieval ideas, which although they began to lose ground by the end of the sixteenth century, still had some supporters at the beginning of the nineteenth century. For them a child should behave in the same way as an adult — and not play any more boisterously than Mlle de Condé had done. These views certainly were out-of-date. Throughout the nineteenth century the right and the duty of children to play their own games, instead of the adult games they had shared until then, were upheld. For about thirty years girls' pantalettes had a symbolic value; they signified childhood. In Parisian society childhood stopped at the age of eleven. This is the kind of advice given by the *Journal des Demoiselles* in the middle of Louis-Philippe's reign: "If your sister is making her first communion at Easter, this is how she should be dressed for that most beautiful day of her life: in a long white silk dress. It must be long because mama will not allow a little girl to wear trousers the day she

ENCORE UNE CRINOLINE !!!!!

participates in the most august religious act." If the writer insisted that the dress must be long it was because trousers had permitted children's dresses to be made shorter, thus also accentuating the difference from adults'. Girls' dresses were made shorter throughout the nineteenth century. The Comtesse de Ségur's daughters wore their dresses to the calf, and their legs were hidden by pantalettes down to the ankles. By 1913 girls showed their knees.

In town girls were dressed as young ladies after their first communion, but not so among the lower middle classes in the provinces who prolonged childhood. They felt the need to distinguish themselves from the working class by all possible means. The working classes followed the old order which counted children as adults from a very early age and did not give them different clothes; they also sent children out to work very young. To show the difference, the lower middle class kept its daughters as children until the age of seventeen or eighteen, when they still thought babies were found under gooseberry bushes, whereas their grandmothers knew the answer to this question at

the age of five. Under Charles X and Louis-Philippe the foundations were laid for a society that would need Freud by the end of the century. The innocent young girl (who never existed under the old regime) wore children's trousers as long as possible, and to leave them off was equivalent to getting married. In one story, a young girl whose engagement is broken off cries: "Now I shall always have to wear trousers!"

Such an exclamation might lead one to believe that women still wore nothing under their petticoats at the end of the eighteenth century, but this is only half-true.

In England trousers were worn by the upper classes, and there was even rivalry between pantaloons and drawers. Aristocrats like the Duchess of Bedford, Lady Charlotte Lindsey, flaunted them even in the street. On the beach, for bathing, they were inescapable. Pantaloons, reserved for the ruling classes, were defended also by the progressionist ladies. However, they did not wear them all the time, and usually put on drawers that did not show below the dress and were unsuspected by the public.

In France drawers were still worn only by dancers. Other women who wore trousers made sure they were very visible; they were embroidered, scalloped, frilled, cut low over the instep and held down with understraps decorated with gold buttons. When were they worn? Some working girls put them on to do jobs where

Left: Manufacture of crinolines, fitting the hoops, 1860s. The production of these accessories had become a major industry. Technical advances reduced the manufacturing costs and brought them within the reach of all social levels, which may be one of the reasons why it began to lose favour among the fashionable classes. The change occurred around 1865: wide circles became ovals and came down towards the knees, the natural shape of the hips reappeared and the fullness of the skirt shifted towards the back.
Below: Advertisement for garters and "Parisian buckles", Paris, 1862. The garter predominated until the end of the century, but around 1862 we find suspenders made of ribbons passed through buckles attached to the stockings.
Far left: One more Crinoline, humorous pictures, 1860s.

their modesty might be compromised. Among the middle classes they were worn more and more for sports, although not for bathing. They were also worn for riding and for travelling. The comment of the fashion journal *La Mésangère* that trousers were fashionable "for children and young girls" but that "if women wore them regularly, it must be because they had ugly legs", held good until the beginning of the Second Empire. This concern about legs was all the more serious because skirts were being made much fuller and more rounded, and copying those of the little girls, they were now shorter and showed the bottom of the calf. *La Mésangère* added that women should only wear trousers in certain circumstances: "How would a lady dare ride a horse or a donkey or sit on a swing without the protection of this garment?" Not only had the king's sword been replaced by a middle-class umbrella, but middle-class prudery prevailed everywhere, and no lady could have a fall like the ones that made Louis XIV laugh so much.

These considerations might well have led to women wearing some form of trousers all the time from 1830 onwards, had the situation been as simple as this. The most important opposition came from the clergy, who never shared the opinion that trousers would assure women's modesty. They thought trousers were evil for three reasons: first they might encourage women to behave much

more freely; second they were particularly suspicious because they originated in the Napoleonic regime; and third they were approved by dangerous revolutionaries like Saint-Simon and Cabet. The former regarded the universal adoption of trousers by women as a decisive step in their emancipation; the latter praised their virtue in the *Voyage en Icarie*. In view of this, it is not difficult to understand why at the end of Louis-Philippe's reign, trousers were prohibited even in the school outfits of the Ursuline nuns' boarders. This was not the last time conservative elements opposed a new garment, even though it contributed to propriety. Even today schoolgirls may meet with similar opposition if they want to wear trousers in winter instead of a skirt.

There was yet one other reason that carried just as much weight: the shorter fashions of the bourgeois monarchy gave pretty women a chance to have their legs admired, and they were not particularly keen to hide them in trousers.

But from 1840 dresses were longer, and the feet were hidden. A woman who wore trousers no longer risked being suspected of hiding a deformity. As dresses grew longer they also grew wider and finally the crinoline, a frame of wooden and then iron hoops, took over the role abandoned eighty years earlier by the pannier, and two hundred and fifty years earlier by the farthingale.

Like the pannier and the farthing-ale, the crinoline was fastened round the waist and held the skirts out, so a woman had two contradictory arguments in favour of wearing trousers. On the one hand, her dress swept the floor and concealed her ankles, so by

covering these with trousers she was not hiding them further. On the other hand, the crinoline was so stiff that when going downstairs she only had to lean backwards a little to be showing her legs up to her knees. So trousers once more safeguarded her modesty. Another argument was the example of American women: from 1851 bloomerism (named after Mrs. Amelia Bloomer) was all the rage:

that is a short skirt over long trousers.

Even without all these excellent reasons I think trousers would eventually have caught on, simply because of one great characteristic of the modern period: children's clothes always end up being worn by adults. Mothers were bound to start wearing pantalettes like their daughters wore, just as from 1830 fathers had stopped wearing breeches and dressed instead in the trousers small boys had been wearing since the reign of Louis XVI.

This precept of the nineteenth and early twentieth centuries brought up another: the style of clothing became more working class. These two trends were linked, because at first parents had amused themselves by dressing their children in peasant, workman and military styles, and so when they copied the children's clothes they were getting closer to working class clothes. This is confirmed by the blue jeans and leather garments worn today.

Women's pantaloons and drawers spread to the suburbs and even to working-class women, although these hardly ever wore crinolines. They were a symbol of propriety. A girl in drawers showed her virtue, one without her drawers her forwardness. Peasant women were the only ones who did not know about the new garment, and in certain regions, as we shall see, it remained unknown till the present. Among the aristocracy drawers were still not worn consistently for another fifteen years or so. They were worn for a grand dinner, or to go boating on the

Left: Bloomers, U.S.A., 1851. The bloomerist style usually favoured trousers which more or less matched the skirt; they cannot therefore strictly be called underwear. On the other hand, the pantaloon fashion spreading through Europe involved a material similar to that of the skirt or chemise, but quite unrelated to the overgarment, so that it became an item of lingerie, real "underwear".

Seine, or to travel the Pyrenees on a mule in the summer for example, but on an ordinary day ladies quite often did not bother to put them on.

At first this under-garment was in no way considered erotic in men's eyes; in fact, they detested it. In his *Mémoires* Viel-Castel remarked on the bad taste of a marchioness who arrived at a lovers' rendezvous protected by drawers — worse still, by fastened drawers. Victor-Emmanuel got furious at the mention of pantalettes because they prevented him from seeing women's ankles and this made him unhappy. A cartoon which appeared in 1863 showed the grandstand at a racecourse during a sudden rain shower, with the legend: "There used to be pretty legs to take your mind off the rain, now there's only trousers and macadam."

The motivation behind wearing trousers during the Second Empire was in no way the same as during the Renaissance. There was no question of showing more than the frilled bottoms, nor were they used as an excuse for greater freedom of movement. They were made of light material, the same as chemises and petticoats, and quite different from ordinary dress material. Although they wore trousers, the women of the Second Empire were not for a moment thinking of thwarting the evolution of different clothes for the two sexes. Yet the men were not wrong in suspecting a slight desire for defence on the part of the women. The Empress Eugenie and her friends came

out in favour of the new underwear in the hope that it would give the court a good reputation. In short, they succumbed to the Victorian tyranny that was to crush the second half of nineteenth century.

In England this underwear had become obligatory. It was correct, and therefore imperative, to wear it every day. So, because of their Anglomania, French women started to think of trousers as a necessity instead of a gimmick. In return, the English who until then had preferred drawers and been very fond of flannel, went wild about pantalettes *à la française*, made of satin and decorated with lace frills. They were practical, and preferred their trousers open and buttoned, but in France competition between open trousers and sewn-up ones like the little girls wore, was already fierce. At the fall of the Empire it was no longer a question of whether or not a woman wore trousers, but of how they were made. The religious boarding schools that had forbidden them twenty years earlier now made them compulsory under the name of "modesty hose". This was a good name for an under-garment that had been created neither out of extravagance or sensuality, nor from a real desire for comfort. Women were starting to sink into the respectable seclusion that was their lot throughout the century — just compare the dignified, formal ladies painted by Winterhalter with the carefree bold-eyed ladies with bare legs sketched by Tiepolo or Watteau.

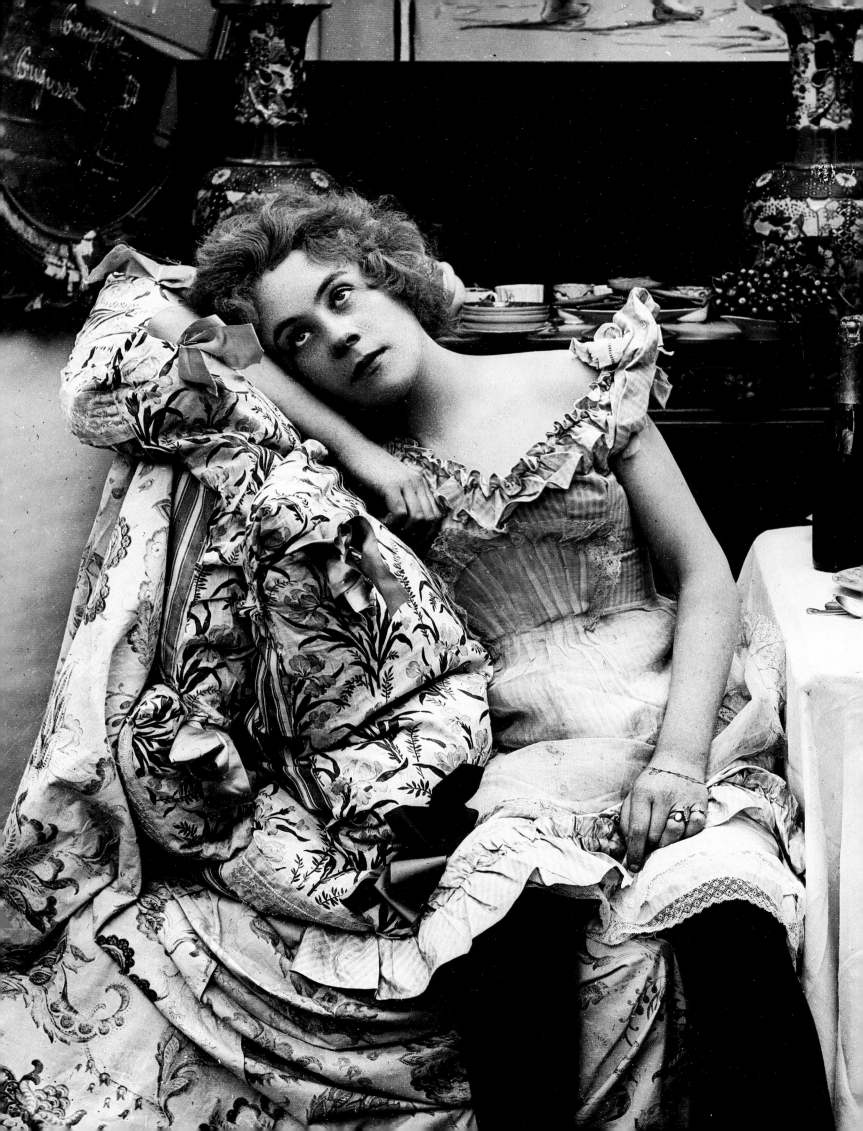

F R E U D ' S
P A T I E N T S

The crinoline disappeared soon after Napoleon III's surrender to the Germans in 1870. It had reigned for fifteen years. We do not know why it came into being, but we know how: at the end of a movement that started with the death of Louis XV. From 1775 to 1800 shapes, whether in architecture, furniture or clothes, had tended to lose their roundness and become elongated, straight and light; from 1800 to 1820 they were still guided by the same principles but did not observe them

scrupulously, so all the lines became heavier; between 1820 and 1850 they returned to cambers and curves, with narrowness as a contrast; after 1850 the reaction was even more evident, furniture being a straight imitation of the Louis XV style and the crinoline copying the pannier. The movement had gone full circle. This seemed to apply to politics too, for only one or two euphemisms in the constitution of Napoleon III disclosed that the Revolution had ever taken place.

At the beginning of the movement

Photo taken from a saucy magazine, Paris 1900.
Left: Courtesan in chemise and drawers, circa 1900.

we have the Louis XV woman, weighed down with underwear (chemise, petticoat, corset) beneath the bell-shaped pannier. In the trough of the wave is the woman of the Directory, straight as a pillar, and almost denuded of underwear. Then on the next crest we find the woman of the Second Empire, once more corseted and buried beneath a bell-like structure, once more composed of domes and curves.

The crinoline was much more vast than the pannier, falling closer to the ground and imprisoning women in a hemisphere. The corset also was much longer than at the time of Louis XV and even crushed the thighs. If its cup-shaped supports did not crush the breasts too much, it was because the fashion was for the breast to be low, and the shoulders drooped, like the Empress's. With the help of several maids a fashionable woman put on a long chemise, had herself laced into a long corset, climbed into enormous pantaloons that puffed out the bottom of her chemise. Then she was pushed between the hoops of the crinoline and the petticoats were put over it.

Nor could he have foreseen that the crinoline would disappear more quickly than the pannier and the farthingale did. Since clothes are not a necessity, it is difficult to predict their evolution. In the nineteenth century Tocqueville declared that in the twentieth century the two great powers would be America and Russia;

in 1919 Jacques Bainville predicted war would break out in 1939 and that it would be because of the Danzig corridor. I suggest that even if Tocqueville and Bainville had been interested in clothes as they were in the political relations between the great powers, they would have been wrong if they had tried to predict the evolution of a petticoat. In 1880 Robida published his science fiction book called *The Twentieth Century* in which he predicted television, the helicopter, and even popular tourism — but he dressed his heroines in zouave trousers and veiled tricorns. Under the authoritarian Empire there was not the slightest indication that the crinoline was to disappear so soon. On the contrary, the industry of the furniture-makers and coach-builders in making seats and doors designed to admit this garment,

The Box, or the Attractions of the Bustle. J. Béraud, circa 1883. <u>Below</u>: Bustle, Warner model, U.S.A., 1880s. The French defeat at Sedan in 1870 marked the end of crinolines which were replaced by the bustle, an accessory which accentuated the rear. Two skirts were worn: one hung straight down, the other was gathered at the back in a voluminous draping, called the *pouf*, and held up by the half-cage suspended below the waist — the bustle. Towards the close of the century, it was reduced to a small cushion attached to the waist. <u>Left</u>: The crinoline in daily life, 1860s.

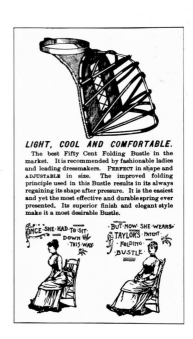

LIGHT, COOL AND COMFORTABLE.
The best Fifty Cent Folding Bustle in the market. It is recommended by fashionable ladies and leading dressmakers. PERFECT in shape and ADJUSTABLE in size. The improved folding principle used in this Bustle results in its always regaining its shape after pressure. It is the easiest and yet the most effective and durable spring ever presented. Its superior finish and elegant style make it a most desirable Bustle.

·ONCE·SHE·HAD·TO·SIT· DOWN ·THIS·WAY·
·BUT·NOW· SHE·WEARS· TAYLOR'S·PATENT· ·FOLDING· ·BUSTLE·

Corset, English model, 1879-1880. <u>Below</u>: Detail of the same corset, with back laced up. The metal eyelet, invented around 1828, was a great improvement on the simple holes that had been cut into the material and then inadequately protected by buttonhole stitching. Nevertheless, in the luxury trade where a perfect finish was the rule, the metal eyelet was overembroidered by hand. <u>Right</u>: Medical corset. American model, 1890.

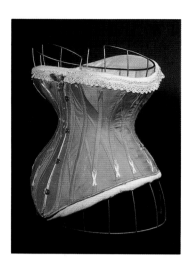

suggested that it would last for ever.

Although the crinoline disappeared suddenly the reaction that followed it was the same as that which followed the disappearance of the pannier and the farthingale: in the seventeenth and eighteenth centuries women had put on more petticoats and worn padding round their hips, and at the beginning of the Third Republic they resorted to a tournure to enhance their bottoms.

At first this bustle was a small pad of horsehair or several layers of stiff material. Then later it became a framework of metal rings secured with bands of cloth. It looked rather like a cage suspended from the small of the back between the petticoat and the dress. Part of the skirt was lifted like a curtain and draped over the hump made by the cage.

The encumbering crinoline had disappeared, but women were still not able to move freely. On the contrary, from the time of the Franco-Prussian war until World War I women remained strapped in. Over the chemise they wore a corset that strangled them from the shoulders to the thighs. The bottom of the corset was hidden by wide drawers into which the bottom of the chemise was tucked. The top was covered by a camisole, embroidered and scalloped like the drawers. Several petticoats were tied round the waist. The role of the corset was to restrict the bust and the hips; the role of the skirt was to make the tangle of petticoats, che-

Wind gust, 1890.
The bustle and the
hobble skirt (see below)
made way for the 1900
silhouette: close-fitting
bodice, bell-shaped skirt
hugging the hips. Once
again, woman was at the
mercy of the wind.
However, "in olden times
the wind bared the most
secret of charms: today it
offers to all eyes great
displays of white and
lace". (*Le Charivari*,
1899). The presence of
the "pantaloons", fifty
years after its adoption,
still aroused a few
lingering regrets.

mise, drawers, suspenders, garters, stockings, boots and the hump of the bustle on the buttocks, fit as tightly as possible round the legs. The skirt was so narrow and long that a woman's thighs were riveted together when she walked. She could only move from the knees down, and even then not very much.

From the Athens of Pericles to the Paris of the Second Empire, dresses had remained more or less capricious, more or less revealing, more or less flowing, more or less easily hitched up. At the beginning of the Third Empire none of these epithets applied to them any longer. These dresses were not only almost hermetically sealed, but the underwear beneath them provided further ramparts against improbable assaults. The petticoats clung to the drawers which in their turn were caught up with the chemise and the corset, and were finally bastioned by the bustle.

As if they could have been a breach in these defences, the slits in drawers tended to disappear or be made shorter. Quite often they were just left at the back to fit more easily over the chemise. A long slit was found only in the country or in Paris in the clothes of working women or prostitutes. Sewing-girls make their little trousers in the manner of loose women "semi-transparent, and so funny with their long, long slits". In any case there was no question of any prying eyes seeing the bottom of any drawers, because the skirt hid every-

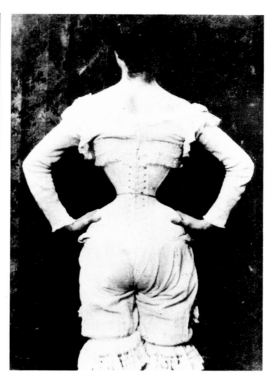

thing down to the boots.

Maybe in the fraction of a second while a woman was getting on to a bus, an experienced observer would glimpse the tops of the boots. It could be said that at this period boots became underclothes. The fetishists were not mistaken. In earlier times a woman's foot in a shoe had an erotic significance. The shoe more than any other article of clothing had disturbed a writer like Restif de la Bretonne. But these infatuations had always remained isolated, and it was not until the Third Republic that fetishism was really born, of an almost morbid intensity, and directed above all at boots and corsets.

No one should study Freud's work without taking into consideration the period in which he lived. The repres-

The wasp-waist, late 19th century. In 1904, a certain Dr Chapotot gave an account of the misfortunes of a coquette: "Mlle J-, age 17, had worn a tight brassiere at the age of 10. At 12 she wore a corset which she laced up much more tightly than one does at that age. She was uncomfortable and already felt the need to unlace after a meal. From 14 to 15, in spite of the pain, she persisted in her aim of having a very thin waist. It was not long before she suffered acute pains in the epigastrium which lasted all day and ceased only when she took off her corset."

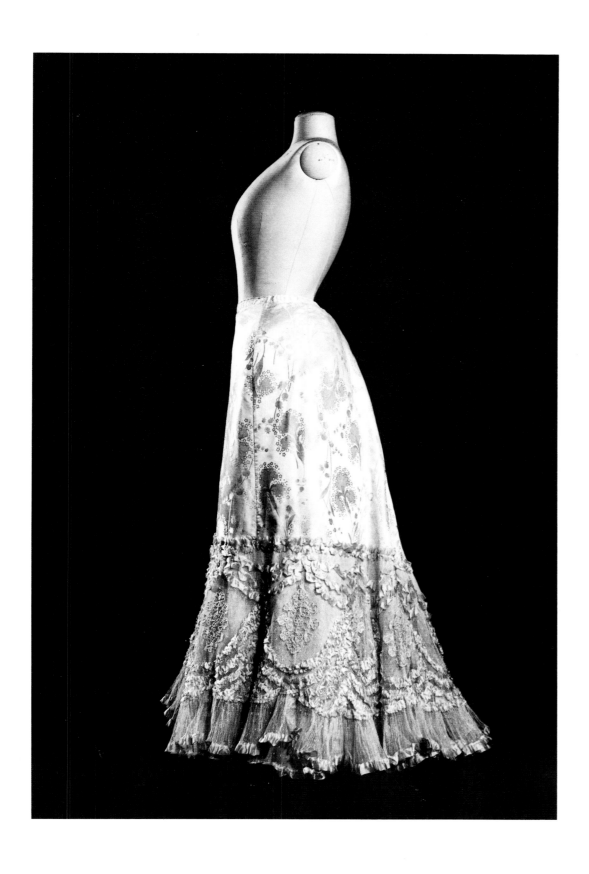

French petticoat, circa 1900, black faille silk. Chantilly lace flounces on a background of white taffeta, black faille bows.

Below: Postcard, part of a set showing the various stages of a young milliner's toilet, circa 1900. The caption indicates clearly that suspenders have now replaced garters which the heroine considers old-fashioned.

Far left: Corset, French model, circa 1896. White satin decorated with pink eglantines. The shape of this busk which curves forward will be replaced in 1900 by a new line: the straight-front corset.

DESSUS ET DESSOUS

Striptease by a
music hall artiste, taken
from a saucy magazine.
Paris, 1900.

sions he analysed were almost certainly peculiar to this particular moment in the history of clothing when clothes seemed to be intended to confine and enclose the female body, when for the first time the purpose of underwear seemed to be to prevent amorous overtures, which could not have failed to disturb Freud's patients.

One of Pierre Louÿs novels expounds in great detail the obsession at once delightful and oppressive, by which men are held because of the defensive features of women's underwear. In *La Femme et le Pantin* after the moral and emotional obstacles have been overcome, the admirer comes up against all the cloth, straps and fasteners the woman is done up in, for fear of arousing desires. That a whole novel should be devoted to this theme is some indication of the part underwear played in the formation of eroticism. Desire was an emotion that had to be endured for a long time; it was prolonged and increased by the number of layers that foiled it.

Strip-tease, which is quite the reverse of a sudden inspiration, also had to take a long time. It must have started at the end of the nineteenth century. And stripping is exactly what happened, but at first it was called *coucher* — bedtime. The whole of Paris went to see the *Coucher d'Yvette*. To the music of a piano a woman in day clothes appeared on the stage set of a bedroom, and slowly started to take off her clothes. Her

underclothes were simple, even ordinary, she used only what she normally wore in the daytime. Although it aroused the audience, the show remained ingenuous and Yvette always managed to put her nightdress on without being seen naked, and slip into bed as the curtain went down. Then there would be similar rituals showing Yvette getting up and Yvette preparing to take a bath. Finally, at the Folies-Bergère, the Casino de Paris and similar places, by 1893 there was nothing but shows like "The lady wakes up", "The Parisian dressing-room" and the ever-popular "Hunt the flea". At the end of the century, when women were mummified by their clothes, a number of suggestive magazines appeared, with lots of drawings of women's underwear that could be savoured at length. Nudity was not neglected either. After 1900 it appeared on the stage at the Folies-Pigalle, then all over Paris, and all over Europe. Up to 1914 the success of these strip shows which ended in nudity continued to actuate critics and newpaper reporters, and to delight the public — which was quite understandable, for although fashion had changed between 1890 and 1914, the forbidding underwear still remained.

Today we are used to nude dancers in the shows in Montmartre. At the beginning of the century they were revolutionary, and can only be explained by the obsession to which

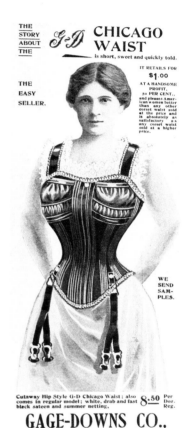

Advertisement for corsets in the *Women's and Infants' Furnisher*, U.S.A., 1898.
Left: Corset, brocaded silk, cream-coloured with embroidery and lace flounces in matching shades. American model, 1895. Boxes with brand advertisements (circa 1895) by two leading corset manufacturers: C.P. Corsets, A La Sirène, France, and C/B Corsets a la Spirite, United States.

men were driven because of the excessive number of clothes women wore. It was quite a break with the tradition that forbade nudity in dance. In Egypt and Greece dancers were naked only because beautiful

Louis XIV or St. Louis or Napoleon. There have always been orgies, even in the Vatican, but they would never have led to a daily show available to everyone. By the first decade of this century the middle classes must have

figures were admired and nudity had not yet acquired scandalous overtones. When clothes became the rule in the towns, they were in the theatres too. Parisians would never have gone to see a nude show under

been at the end of their tether to go and look for excitement publicly.

The change in dress in 1890 had modified the female form, but it had not made it any freer. The bustle had disappeared, but instead of reverting

Advertisements for corsets in the *Women's and Infants' Furnisher*, U.S.A., 1898.

to straight dresses as they did from the reign of Louis XVI to the Directory, women became S-shaped.

As usual the change in women's dress corresponded to a change in furniture. There was the same resemblance between a Directory chair and a woman in a tunic as between the S-shaped woman of 1900 and the S of table legs and art nouveau decorations.

To achieve the S-shape women had to endure another cruel new corset. In front it had long metal stays that did not just flatten the stomach, but crushed it. The bottom of the corset cut into the groin, so that the wearer had to pull in the small of the back to be comfortable. It fastened with hooks, and was still worn over the chemise which was stretched very tightly because it had to support the breasts. The bottom of the chemise was still tucked into the drawers which had been getting shorter since 1870 and were now just a sort of sack with two short legs.

In this corset women in 1900 had a large behind, crushed their stomachs almost vertically, and threw their bust out as far as it would go. Still bound and sealed up, more crippled and crushed than ever, women in 1900 just looked strange. From their appearance it seemed that they had no spinal column or abdomen, only an enormous behind, in short they looked even less human than women did in the farthingale. It is not hard to see why the sight of them increased the number of Freud's patients.

In this setting, the popular *Coucher d'Yvette* played the reassuring role of an initiating ceremony, designed to show school-boys that as a woman took off her clothes she revealed a body that differed in certain ways from a man's, but was not as radically different as it seemed.

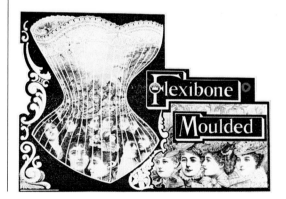

THE STRICTURES
OF MORALITY

By the end of the Regency the French realized that fashion was synonymous with change, and was dependent on taste, like art and literature. They also knew they were imaginative enough never to lack inspiration, and so they imposed their ideas about clothes throughout Europe. From time to time they welcomed some innovation from abroad, Frenchified it eagerly, only showing themselves so liberal because they were all-powerful.

This empire often annoyed the Anglo-Saxons. At first they rebelled against every new French garment, then they accepted it, usually just as it was going out of fashion in Paris, and became dominated by it to the extent that they would defend a garment they had once detested. From the beginning of the eighteenth century Parisian women amused themselves examining the clothes of a foreigner who had just arrived, and their amusement was all the more annoying to the person who was the object of it because it was based on

WARNER'S
RUST-PROOF CORSETS

EVERY PAIR GUARANTEED

1902.

the quiet certainty of infallibility.

In America, in England, in Germany they had laughed at the pannier, looked down on the bustle, treated the crinoline as if it were the devil's invention, and now from one capitulation to the next, they were about to surrender abjectly to the S-shaped corset.

Nevertheless the two hundred year long battle against the authority of Paris, had toughened and armed the northern women and driven them to organization. From the eighteenth century groups of women got together in Germany to combat the plagues that spread from France. They had not succeeded against the *cul,* but undeterred kept a close watch on the crinoline. They were defeated once again, and enlisted the help of caricaturists to oppose the tournure which was christened "satan's tool", "servant of vice" and portrayed as a divan for men to sit on. In the United States the moralizing associations realized there was no point in criticizing, and instead tried to create rational clothes of which the best known were bloomers. But when the S-shaped corset appeared, all over northern Europe and the United States the cry went up: "conquer fashion!"

And to conquer it they thought of making dress more masculine. In the second half of the nineteenth century it was chiefly the socialists and Pro-

Straight front corset. English design, 1903. Black satin with white overstitching and mixed whalebone and steel ribbing.
Left: Examples of fine jewellery. Hooks to attach underwear to corsets and de luxe garters, from the periodical *Les Dessous Elégants,* Paris, 1904. The fasteners were of chiselled gold or silver set with opals or rubies with baroque pearl pendants. The garters were of crimped elastic to match the corset, with hooks of enamelled gold set with emeralds and white pearls.
Far left: Warner advertisement, United States. From the late nineteenth century steel was competing with buffalo horn and whalebone, but rust was a problem. Warners then patented the famous "rust-proof corset".

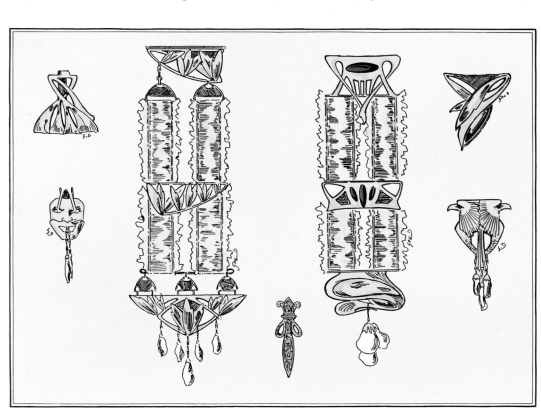

Longer, shorter, with a narrower or a more relaxed waist, the corset never stopped evolving from 1900 to the First World War. Every season corsetmakers established, down to the minutest detail, the inflexible rules of fashion. The new style of 1904 included: the handpainted corset (fig. 5), black banished in favour of pastel shades with luxuriant motifs — branches of white lilac over blue satin (fig. 6), lilies and monochrome foliage on a green background (fig. 1), golden skin gloves (fig. 4), a petticoat or a chemisette to match the corset (fig. 2), while the boudoir gown, shown here in pink silk (fig. 3) was not subject to rules: anything was acceptable.

1

2

5

3

4

6

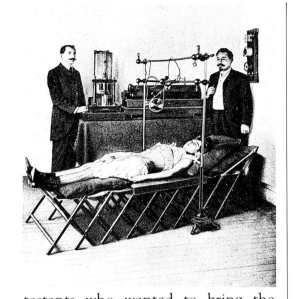

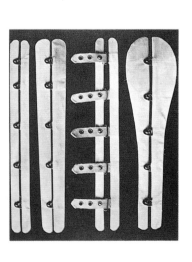

testants who wanted to bring the style of dress of the two sexes closer together. In the 1848 Revolution the followers of Saint-Simon had already suggested a female uniform of cloth trousers. Bloomers appeared in Europe at the same time as the crinoline and only succeeded in causing amusement, even in London where they were caricatured in *Punch*. But in 1893 when Paris fashion had reached the height of absurdity, resorting to masculine styles seemed to be based on sound sense. In the United States, Miss Annie Miller organized many clubs advocating "dress reform" and in Germany there were the *Reform-Bien-Kleider*. In England, Lady Bective launched the divided skirt which shocked London, and provoked the intervention of the police in Madrid. Even more extreme, in Paris Mme Astyé de Valsere put forward a bill to the Chamber of Deputies to allow

women to dress in men's clothes. The police took this up at once and kept a close watch on her.

The reformist ladies tried to suppress the corset and change the skirt for trousers in the name of morality, but the conservative forces that maintained that men wore trousers and women dresses also did so in the name of morality, which did not help to simplify matters. Particularly in the Latin countries where the middle classes were catholic and republican any attempt to reform female costume was considered scandalous. It is significant that in France it was the bourgeoisie in power during the Directory who decreed that a woman wearing masculine clothes had to get special authorization from the Minister of the Interior. It was given to the army's provision suppliers, girls doing manual work, and prostitutes who had turned respectable. George Sand got permission, so did Marguerite

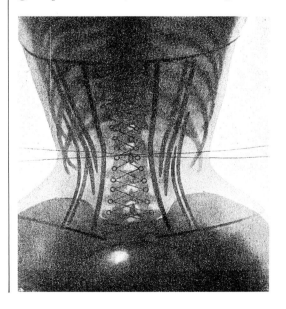

Bellanger because she wanted to visit her lover Napoleon III, without attracting attention, so did Mme Dieulafoir because she was an explorer.

Mme Astyé de Valsere's followers were refused permission, and were arrested in the streets of Paris. The police discovered that amongst these virtuous reformers there were some prostitutes who had only taken to wearing trousers to attract attention. Public opinion then concluded that any attempt women made to change their habitual dress was occasioned by a taste for debauchery.

Only cycling bloomers came out of the affray if not conquerors, at least tolerated, and this only if the person wearing them proved she was a cyclist, either by riding or by pushing her machine. Cycling bloomers were vast and baggy and took care not to suggest any shape; they were inspired by ordinary bloomers, by the divided skirt and by oriental costume. They were stared at and were the object of ribald songs and suggestive captions to titillating drawings. Many young girls were not allowed to wear them. By 1900 male obsession was such that it seized on anything: a garment that was supposed to be practical and sensible was turned into an erotic symbol.

Although they were made of coarse cloth, cycling bloomers looked like drawers that women had finally consented to show. In addition, at a time when clothes and underclothes enveloped a woman and veils, gloves and muffs were used to hide what little of her body escaped the dress, the sight of these cyclists in bloomers, gripping the saddle between their

LES DESSOUS ÉLÉGANTS
8, Rue Halévy. PARIS.

Camisole, French style, around 1904. White buckram, lace insertion in a herringbone pattern, satin-stitch embroidery, pink satin ribbons.
Right: Wedding set, consisting of a combination (fig. 1), a day chemise (fig. 2) and French-style knickers, 1909. Buckram with small pleats, satin-stitch embroidered garlands and monograms, insertion and flounces of Irish lace, and interwoven pink satin ribbon.
Far right: Chemise, French model from around 1911.

1

2

3

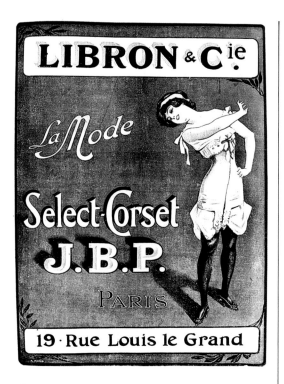

LIBRON & Cie.
La Mode
Select-Corset
J.B.P.
PARIS
19 · Rue Louis le Grand

thighs, aroused men violently.

It would not be strictly accurate to say that the graceful way in which women had adapted trousers led to their being freed of the S-shaped corset so soon; but it is a fact that even though the reformist clubs of the twentieth century were as powerless as the sumptuary laws of the fifteenth when it came to changing fashions, sport did give birth to clothes that were quite quickly adapted for everyday wear.

Men's hunting, driving, yachting and golf clothes all became acceptable in a drawing room or office. This had nothing to do with convenience, but was a form of snobbism. When he left his boat a yachtsman kept his blazer and cap on as long as possible as a status symbol, and thus prompted

imitators who had never been anywhere near a yacht.

But cycling soon became a popular sport and no one could expect to attract attention by wearing bloomers. So women's clothes evolved more in the style of holiday wear — holidays were still the privilege of a certain section of the middle classes. Tennis required a shorter dress, flat shoes, a loose corset: mountain climbing, cloth trousers.

Conservative elements in society tried hard to prevent women dressed for these sports appearing anywhere but on the tennis court or mountain side. But out of vanity these women wanted to show that they had just been climbing or playing tennis, and they braved social censure all the more easily because they belonged to the upper class. An example set by the upper class is soon followed. After spending the holidays in a light skirt, it was quite natural to want to wear the same sort of comfortable clothes in town.

Another development already mentioned led to a revolution in costume: adults started to copy children's dress. Little girls do not wear corsets; their skirts came to the knee and under them they wore such short drawers that they were really knickers — which women were to adopt later.

Nevertheless the transformation would not have been quite so rapid without the intervention of other important factors. In the first place fashion was to change, for that is its

"No Clasps to Grip the Hose and Rip"

145

essence. The S-shape no longer met with the approval of a generation that was moving away from the 1900 style, and getting back to straight lines by way of cubism. In 1893 after the tournure disappeared women and furniture should have gone back to straight lines as they did when the *cul* went out of fashion. They were prevented by the serpentine shape of the turn of the century.

Slowly the corset became straight again and did not force women's bodies into a curve, but it was not abolished completely. The pale washed-out colours were replaced by bright one. Ankles were visible again.

Materials were becoming lighter, skirts were getting shorter, and this would have gone on happening slowly, if a pistol shot had not been fired in Sarajevo on 28 June 1914. The history of ladies' underwear also confirms that the 1918–1918 war was, as Lenin said, a period complete in itself, and that as well as being a war, it was a revolution.

WORLD WAR I

*I*t would be an exaggeration to say that skirts were shortened a couple of inches or that the corset shrank back to the waist the moment the first cannon was fired at the beginning of August 1914. During the first months of the war, neither fashion nor the way of life changed. The Kaiser, Joffre, and the women were all agreed on one point: the fighting would be over by Christmas. By Christmas the armies were dug in to the trenches, and the war was no longer an event, but was becoming a

habit. This habit brought with it a new way of life which was reflected in women's underwear. The old order defended itself but it was shaky. The Czar did not abdicate until 1917; the corset gave up its empire in 1915.

Holidays and sports had already paved way for a change in women's clothes, and the war did the rest. In the country the women went to work in the fields and started to drive vans; in the towns they worked in the factories; among the middle classes it was considered socially acceptable to

The soldier look, circa 1917.
Left: Corset or "belt" front-laced over a chemise with embroidery and appliqué lace. Gossard, England, 1920.

Woman at her toilet, France, 1915. This silhouette in the *Parisienne* shows how underwear had become simplified, a trend which began in 1890 and grew in importance under the influence of the designer Paul Poiret. His vision of the woman conflicted with the "fattening" proliferation of underclothes. The short "drawers" foreshadowed the appearance of knickers, the underskirt disappeared, the chemise was shortened. Finally, Poiret urged the banishment of all artificial paraphernalia. <u>Below</u>: Combination camisole-knickers, French model, 1917. White nainsouk with Valencienne lace insertions, attached to sky blue ribbons.

become a nurse or to drive an ambulance. Uniforms were changing at the Front and at home women changed their shape and adopted new quick and efficient, military-like gestures. In Paris the "soldier" style caught on so quickly that the women who had gone to the country on holiday were conspicuous when they returned because of all the make-up and feathers they wore. The first men home on leave did not recognize the Parisian women. Many authors wrote about it, including Colette: "I arrived at the *gare de l'Est* excited, trembling, speechless, searching the platform for the girl whose image had not paled in my memory, although I had not seen her for six months: a slim blond girl in a summer dress, her neck and a little of her throat visible in the neck-line of her lawn chemise — a young girl, so feminine, so weak and so brave when we parted ... I was looking for her when a strangled cry called me and I fell into the arms of a youthful second lieutenant who burst into tears against my shoulder. She was dressed in a double-breasted grey-blue overcoat in the latest fashion of the trenches, and her little ears showed beneath a forage of cap trimmed with burnished gold. A stiff dolman collar covered her delicate neck; she had pinned on her breast a Belgian flag and another trinket that she told me straight away was her 'love of 75'. We passed some strangely dressed women in the streets; I even involuntarily saluted a large

lady severely buttoned up in a blue captain's coat, then brushing past a slim corseted young lady I thought I recognized the uniform of the *Cadre noir*. A field-service tunic, dolman, braided cap, why not a bayonet and a rucksack instead of a handbag?"

A fashion which copied the sport of war also reminded women of open air sports, holidays and the comfortable clothes of the beach and the tennis court. Skirts got shorter. On the Boulevards women were suddenly wearing them mid-calf length even though they did not carry a racquet under their arm. They also reduced the corset to a supple girdle that went no higher than the waist and only down to the groin instead of to mid-thigh. Freeing the upper part of the body in this way led to the invention of the brassière. It had in fact existed since 1912 but had never been worn consistently. Women used to wear their corsets over the chemise in such a way that when it was pulled tight it supported their breasts. When the corset was made smaller it could no longer hold the chemise tight enough to support them. The brassière took over. The first brassières were worn over the chemise, but it was quickly seen that the chemise was useless, or at least cumbersome, particularly if it had to go on under the brassière and what remained of the corset, which anyway had by now only served the function of a suspender belt. Soon many women dropped the corset altogether in favour of a suspender belt, and some wore it next to the skin, as they did the brassière.

Now that there was nothing over it the chemise fell to the knee, making a second underskirt. But women's desire to be alert had turned into a passion, so they had to choose between the chemise and the underskirt. They started by making some room under their dresses and left off the frilly bodice or "corset cover" and shortened their drawers. The latter had been designed to cover up the corset from the waist to mid-thighs, and they looked like a sack with two holes for the legs. When there was no more corset to cover and all they had to do was cover the stomach and bottom, like little girls' did, only half as much material was needed. The

heavy lace trimmings were discarded and drawers were made of lighter, thinner materials like lawn and crepe, and also tended to become more transparent. Hitherto they had been black or white; now they were pink. There were two distinct styles: knickers with wide legs that covered several inches of the thighs and knickers with virtually no legs that fitted tightly round the tops of the thighs — forerunners of panties and briefs. The chemise became much shorter until it just barely reached to the knickers. Some were still finished off with a lace flounce, but more and more had just a simple hem. There was still the petticoat between the legs and the skirt, and this justified making the chemise shorter, but not for long — by 1917 many Parisian women stopped wearing petticoats.

Each year of the war skirts got shorter. It was Paris that led the way, but as far away as the Black Sea a French officer on a mission there noted the same phenomenon of shorter skirts. By showing their calves and moving their knees freely woman became much more aware of their legs. They discarded the rather thick lisle stockings they had worn until then, and started wearing silk stockings. The old stockings had been black or white or sometimes coloured; the new ones were flesh coloured. They imitated nudity and made women's legs more like the bare legs of little girls. It seems that women who felt the cold suffered

Advertisement for the Lys brand of stockings, France, 1922. With the war and the shortening of skirts, the days of hosiers who turned out only white or black stockings were numbered. Manufacturers in Paris, Ganges and Troyes had to follow the dictates of fashion and invest in the luxury stocking trade.
Right: Bride's night attire, French model, 1917. The nightdress is narrower toward the ankle, the mantlet and lamp veil are of pink muslin, with gold trim.

when long skirts, underskirts and thick stockings disappeared. Flesh coloured woollen under-stockings that were invisible under the silk were made for them, but they made the legs thicker, so they disappeared very quickly.

Although women had used the war as a pretext to adopt military styles, and their work to shorten their dressed and make their underwear lighter, they had avoided adopting men's clothes. They had amused themselves by copying the trooper's cap and decking it out with frills and braids; in the hospitals they learned to smoke cigarettes; they had played at being foot-soldiers and made themselves more feminine than ever.

Ever since antiquity women doing men's work have always been permitted to wear trousers. In the ambulances at the front some women wore riding breeches and boots under their skirts, particularly those that had occasion to ride — thus following the tradition of the women who supplied the provisions for Napoleon's army. Their example was followed, and shortly after the war the majority of horsewomen gave up riding dresses. The few who kept to them wore breeches underneath.

Many French and Belgian women in occupied territory fought clandestinely for the Allies, crossed the lines secretly, felled forests at night. Some of them found their normal clothes a handicap and although they often kept to their ordinary outer clothes

— a dark costume and a big hat, they put on swimming costumes and tight-fitting knickers underneath to be able to move more easily on their dangerous escapades. But because of the secret nature of their work they did not, however, launch a new fashion.

Nevertheless by the end of the war, any fashion that had not helped free the female body, although still preserving the sexual distinction, was doomed. In the nineteenth century women's bodies had been covered up almost as much as men's. But by 1919 women marked themselves off from men because they had rediscovered their nudity of the eighteenth century, their bodies were again in contact with the air, and likely to be revealed by a gust of wind or a hazardous movement. Women were alone in showing their legs now, men had closed theirs firmly in trousers at the beginning of the nineteenth century. The segregation of clothing had reached its peak.

The differences between boys' and girls' clothes became more marked too. Little boys stopped wearing the skirts they had worn before the war, sometimes until the age of seven. Middle class boys still wore their hair as long as girls until the age of eleven or twelve, but it was cut shorter every year until by the end of the twenties boys' hair was no longer than men's. Similarly lace, silks and colours that men had stopped wearing in the nineteenth century were no longer worn by boys, but only by girls. Boys

Brassiere in mauve taffeta with neutral tone filet lace, corset of mauve satin decorated with flowers, French model, circa 1919.
Right: Brassiere in lemon pongée with lace insertions, lemon satin corset, French model, circa 1920.

Dory

Fisherwomen,
Gironde district, circa
1918. Trousers, as an
over-garment, were still
reserved for work and for
sport.
Below: *The Indiscreet Gale*
L. Peltier.
Right: Muslin pyjamas.
French model, 1920s.
The pyjamas were a
derivation of the male
pyjama but also linked to
the Eastern vogue started
by Art Deco. A novel
form of nightwear, it was
at the same time an
informal house garment
far more convenient than
the *déshabillé*.

could no longer be condemned to wear sky-blue or pink. Women started wearing pyjamas during and immediately after the war, but this should not be construed as an attempt to become mannish. It was quite the reverse: women showed their legs in the street, but coquettishly hid them in private. They had played at being soldiers during the war, and now in the bedroom they played at being young recruits. Besides women's pyjamas showed style and imagination, and were certainly not interchangeable with men's.

Only in sport does the war seem to have had the effect of making things more masculine. Fishing trousers became popular at the same time as riding breeches. So did ski pants and they were worn on excursions in summer as well as winter. They originated in Germany where during the war the police issued many regulations against them. The general who governed Bavaria drew up a decree pages long forbidding women to wear ski pants except on the slopes. The rule we have established that all sports clothes eventually become everyday wear applies to ski pants too, although it took a quarter of a century for them to become popular. They were only widely accepted because they remained an exception. They did not try to replace the dress, nor did they detract from femininity because they were designed to emphasize the rounded lines of the female bottom.

The 1914–1918 war had separated the women from the men but had in no way encouraged them to become mannish. What it had done was to allow them to get rid of the bastions of nineteenth century respectability around their legs and thighs. The cries of the middle-aged when faced with "such unqualified shamelessness" are reminiscent of those of the Russian conservatives when the Bolsheviks took over the Winter Palace. Both were suffering because a page of history had been turned.

Bibi at the Hôtel des Alpes, Chamonix, 1920. Photo: J.H. Lartigue.
Below: Pantaloon-chemise, French design, 1920, black crêpe de Chine edged with pink. In lingerie, black suffered from contradictory judgments from one century to the next, symbolising either virtue or licentiousness. In 1920 it was regarded as acceptably daring.
Far left: Corset Le Select, "invisible under your dress", France 1922. The corset was first jettisoned by the most intrepid women — and the slimmest. Others, in order to conform to a fashion which claimed to be natural while imposing norms of an ideal figure, continued to wear a corset, but a smaller one without whalebones. Above all, discreet and preferably unnoticeable.

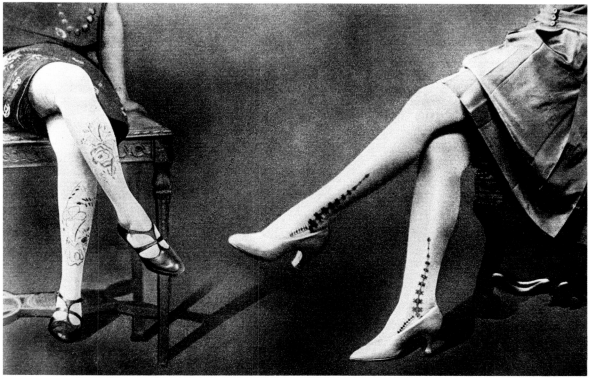

The lingerie section of a large department store, 1920s. <u>Below left</u>: Silk stockings, France, 1920s. The following items were on display in the luxury stocking room of the 1925 Exposition des Arts Décoratifs: gold and silver stockings, stockings decorated with tufts of feathers, stockings embroidered in coloured silks, with diamond bracelets at the ankle or with handsewn pearls. <u>Below</u>: *The Kimono Girl*, Vargas, 1922. The craze for Oriental styles led to the introduction both of the pyjamas and of the kimono, a new version of the dressing-gown. <u>Far left</u>: *Woman With White Stockings*. Valadon, in the 1920s.

INNOCENT OR EXOTIC

Women had never been so closely protected by their clothes as they were in the early years of the Third Republic; they had never been so free, since Athens, as they were in the latter part. A woman who was virtually clad in armour at eighteen, was exposed to the winds in her thirties. No revolution in the history of costume is quite as startling as this one.

In 1928 women wore only a straight flowing dress that hid their breasts and waist and fell to just above the knee. It could be compared to the tunic worn by the Greek women, and their underwear resembled the under-tunic. They wore wide, flowing cami-knickers; the flaps came down to mid-thigh where they were buttoned together. The piece of material that joined them was too narrow and too low to offer any protection, its presence was simply to suggest that the stomach was not really open to the air. But in

Chemise and knickers in ivory silk cloth, insertions by Binche. French model, 1928.
<u>Left</u>: Vamp, 1930.

Cover of *Mode
Pratique*, 7 January 1928.
Below: "Flattener" and
girdle, by Cadolle for
Chanel's 1926 collection.
The "urchin" style which
de-emphasised the bosom
and the hips, required
new accessories: the
"flattener", a long shallow
brassiere which held in
the breasts, and an elastic
knitted girdle, straight
and made in one piece.
Far right: Suspender belts
over cami-knickers.
England, 1928. The
practice of wearing
lingerie under a corset
was on its way out.

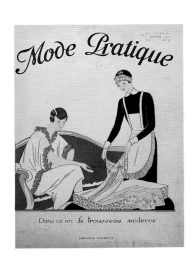

fact women were open to the air up
to the waist and just as freely as the
Greeks were. They no longer even
wore suspender belts; the fashion was
to roll the stockings round garters
above the knee. The only tight-
fitting garment was the brassière,
which girls did not start wearing until
very late, and which many women
decided they did not need anyway.

One might look for the origin of
cami-knickers in the chemises that
were sewn up against patriotic spankings; in a chemise of the period of
Louis-Philippe that buttoned above
the knee, but which disappeared
almost as soon as it was invented; in
an American garment that appeared
at the same time as bloomers, but
which had no success in France
where it was considered "lacking in
modesty and grace"; in the trouser-
combinations that some women wore
about 1870, a sort of petticoat which
had front and back fastened together
with a wide band. But if we study the
purpose of cami-knickers rather than
their appearance it becomes plain
that an analogy with any similar
garment worn in the eighteenth or
nineteenth century is misleading;
from the chemise of the Revolution
to the trouser-combinations the object was to cover up the body and
safeguard modesty, whereas the 1926
model had only a strip of cloth and
swung freely under a short skirt; it
was a ruse to allow women to feel
naked and free whilst superficially
observing the standards of propriety.

The Armoris
for
REAL HEALTH & BEAU

An advocate of
Victorian undergarments
faces two young women
who have cast away their
"deportment" clothes,
England, 1928. The
proper deportment
believed to be the result
of a corseted body, was
long associated with
"correct" female
behaviour.
<u>Below</u>: Transparency and
semi-nudity are features
of this Poiret model
devised for a fancy dress
party. 1920s.
<u>Far right</u>: Silk chemise
with lace insertions over
matching loose knickers.
England, 1928.

During the 1920s we note a return to the use of the garter over which the stocking top was rolled back near the middle of the thigh to hold the upper stocking in place. This allowed the minimum of lingerie to be worn under a dress, since even the suspender belt was no longer required. Far right: Lingerie Neyret. France, 1928. Photo: Lipnitzki-Viollet. Following double pages: Frameless bra, girdle of brocaded material with elastic knitted waistbands over silk knickers. Gossard, England, 1930. Fashion settled down from 1928, dresses were longer, the waistline reappeared, the corset was once again mentioned: with a light stiffening of whalebone, laced at the front or the back, it extended fairly well down, while above it continued for 3 or 4 cm beyond the waist. Right: Bra and knickers-suspender belt (attached at the waistline), Gossard, England, 1930.

Artists and caricaturists, who until now had only seen women encased in their clothes, got to work. They gave the woman of 1926 a veiled rather than a clothed body, and then veiled only to mid-thigh, because they took advantage of situations where the woman, sitting down or getting out of a car, showed her bare leg above the stocking rolled round the garter — and the stockings were flesh coloured, getting more and more transparent, closer and closer to complete nudity.

The rolled stocking which looked a bit like a bracelet — the bracelet of the slave — marked that part of the body that was bare to the waist, even to the breasts, for the dress and cami-knickers were not tight-fitting, and so it became an erotic object until the early thirties when suspender belts came back and the garter disappeared.

The 1928 fashion was extreme and so it was bound to revert to earlier ideas. Cami-knickers disappeared almost completely in favour of the camisole and knickers. At this period composite garments reverted to their separate parts, and the parts might then be joined to something else to make another composite garment, and so on.

This change indicated a new trend not only in fashion but also in behaviour. There was a reaction against the licence and free-and-easy ways of 1928 when women had been more or less naked. The little satin

knickers scarcely afforded more protection than the flap of the cami-knickers, but they did preserve the modesty of the wearer rather better. Hair styles and dresses became longer. The time was ripe for panties to take over from knickers.

The soft lace-frilled legs of the knickers were out of keeping with a taste that aspired to bare surfaces and simple lines in furniture and buildings. The tendency to copy children's clothes also led women to wear short well-fitting panties. Sports and holiday clothes were worn more frequently and knickers which might have been revealed by bicycling shorts, stopped being worn in summer — and then in winter too.

Children's panties were made in ribbed cotton, but for adults the silky materials that knickers and been made of, were used. Cotton panties were white or sometimes pink; silk ones pink and occasionally blue. Black underwear which until the war had been worn by respectable women, was now considered of dubious virtue and was worn only by courtesans.

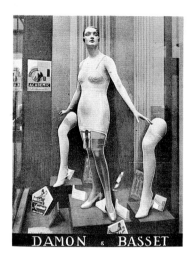

Left, above: Window display, Damon & Basset (metropolitan section, luxury trades), Exposition Coloniale, Paris, 1931. The dummy is wearing a woven "Academic" girdle without elastic thread and a star-shaped bra, finished with crochet.
Above: Display case in the corset department of the Printemps store.
Left: The fitting rooms of Cadolle, specialists in high-class made-to-measure corsetry and underwear, Paris, 1933. Women still preferred their corsets made to measure, whether they went to the leading fashion houses or to their local corset makers who continued to enjoy considerable prosperity. However, the introduction of half sizes brought about a great improvement in ready-made corsets.
Far left: Combination girdle. Water colour by Jean Droit, 1932. This new style was imported from the United States under the name of "corselette".

Combination, Cadolle, Paris, 1935. Triple silk voile with 18-point lace from the Lyons lacemaker Dognin-Racine.

Far left: Combination, Cadolle, Paris, 1934. Silk with lace insertions. The combination was developed around 1880 by joining the chemise to the drawers, then the camisole and the petticoat. This garment achieved its highest level of popularity in the 1920s and became widely used, being almost *de rigueur* until the 1940s.

Catalogue of the
Bon Marche department
store, entitled "Linen
Exhibition. The only one
in the world. Throughout
the month of January".
Paris, 1936. Since the
beginning of the century,
large-scale marketing had
mounted a challenge to
suppliers of female
requirements (house
linen, lingerie) with their

ie et nos pyjamas

policy of seasonal special discounts — the great annual white sales. We should also note that during the 1930s in particular there was a rapid downturn in sales of silk lingerie as the result of a switch to artificial and synthetic fibres.

The combinations that the women of 1930 put on over her bra and panties slowly disappeared in the years that led up to World War II. Like knickers they were old-fashioned, and were not suitable for sports or holiday wear. Underwear was heading towards the diminished and strict number of garments — bra, briefs and suspender belt — that was to remain throughout the war.

It is worth noting that women in ancient Rome, in medieval times and in 1914 wore a chemise next to their skin, a simple garment that could easily be washed frequently. By 1940 the women who wore combinations put them on over their bra in the same way they wore their briefs over their suspender belt. In other words they did not mind having rubberized constricting garments that were washed less next to the skin. By the time combinations went out women were prepared to wear dresses and sweaters next to the skin — something hitherto unknown in the history of underwear, which had always been conceived as a necessary layer between the body and outer clothes.

Sensuality had played a big part in ladies' underwear in the last decades of the nineteenth century, but when underwear almost disappeared it had no part left to play. In early times women arouse desire with the idea that they were almost naked under their dresses. The few simple under-garments that they now wore aroused no interest at all. Hence the nostal-

Revue Paris Magazine, France, 1933. Photo: Globe-Perckammer.
Left: Advertisement for Rubis stockings. France, 1936.
Following pages: Three creations by Diana Slip, Paris, 1932. Photo: Schall.

The simplification of feminine underwear gave rise, around 1930, to an erotic craze for Victorian undergarments. The firm of Diana Slip used the skills of corset specialists to develop these superb models which were intended to appeal to a nostalgic and somewhat daring clientèle.

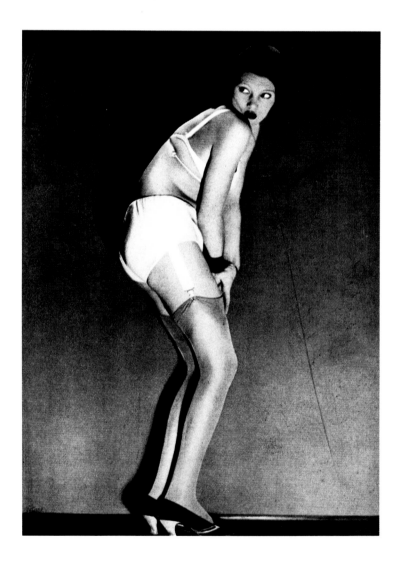

Strapless bra. Prégermain, Paris, 1930s. Photo: Laure Albin Guillot.
Right: Bra and girdle. Gossard, England, 1930s. After the "corsetless" era, women were no longer willing to bear the discomforts of undergarments which were too confining. The manufacturers all endeavoured to improve corsets — now preferably called girdles or belts — increasingly making use of elastic materials. The classical corset became a combination of elastic panels reinforced with brocaded silk or satin.

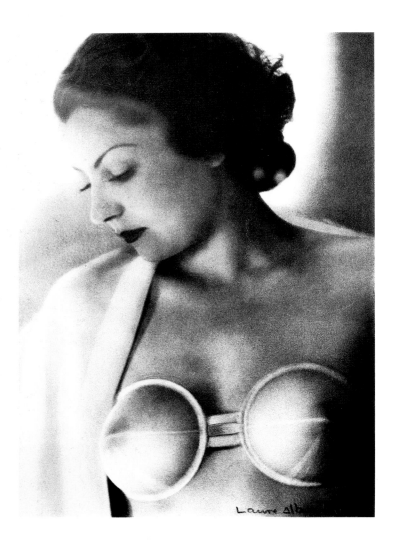

gia that led to the black frilly underwear of the prostitutes, the rustling French can-can drawers worn by the dancers in Montmartre, and the titillating illustrations in magazines. And so at the time when light-coloured briefs were worn, ankle boots, black stockings, corsets and flounces continued to exist rather artificially, kept alive by sensuality. Probably for the first time a cult was made of an out-of-date fashion; one cannot imagine a young man at the time of Louis XIV wanting a revival of Renaissance drawers.

This phenomenon stems from another, much larger, that had gone on growing since the middle of the nineteenth century. The Napoleon III style arose out of a desire to imitate the Louis XV style. But this imitation was not slavish; the furniture-makers used new materials and designs.

It was only shortly after the Franco-Prussian war that the French showed themselves to be lacking in invention. Until the birth of the 1900 style the rich bought any seventeenth or eighteenth-century furniture the antique dealers could lay their hands on, and the poor bought reproductions.

In our own day we have sudden crazes for furniture and even songs from 1900 *la belle époque* or 1926 *les années folles,* so it is not inconceivable that the erotic yearning of the 1930s for Victorian underwear was one of the symptoms of the lack of sensibility found today.

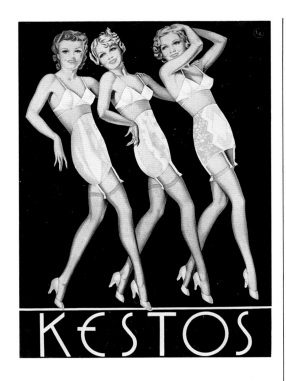

Advertisement for the Kestos brand, France, 1939. Shades in general use during the 1930s were salmon, light coral and pastel pink.
Below: T.G.9, 1933. Photo: Gaston Paris.
Far right: *Two at the Fair.* England, 1938, Photo: Kurt Hutton. This photo exists in several versions. This is the original; on the others the lingerie was retouched in accordance with the prevailing requirements of modesty.

However this return to the past can be justified by one simple fact: for fifty years men had been used to confusing the female body with the underwear that defended it. Even though he might appreciate the light clothes women wore in the street, and the glimpse of the thighs when they sat down, a man of thirty in 1930 felt there was something missing when it came to the intimacy of a conquest. Such straightforward underclothes did not present sufficient obstacles to stir his imagination. *"Couchers d'Yvette"* were no longer in fashion because it was impossible to keep an audience in suspense in front of a woman who only had to take off bra and briefs.

For the return of the strip-tease we have to wait until a generation that had not known underwear before 1914, grew up. From 1933 this group began to show their taste and they opted for briefs. In the magazines that schoolboys swapped they were the underclothes most often shown.

Ingenuous and sturdy little briefs succeeded the complicated, boned, swishing underwear that was both rich and perverse. Sensual love feeds on two extreme emotions. It sometimes requires the will for debauchery to be evident and shameless in the partner, and to be shown in the suggestiveness and quantity of her underwear; sometimes it wants only simple clothes, the sign of an innocence that can be eagerly and pleasurably perverted.

At the time when briefs were considered more sexy than black lace armour, the speed with which this simple garment could be taken off acquired the eroticism that at other times, notably in the Middle Ages and before 1914, had been associated with slow progress over a number of obstacles. In the promiscuous atmosphere of camping, climbing, winter sports or youth hostelling, the ease with which a girl could be taken became exciting. The hero of one of Anouilh's early plays applauds the fact that his young mistress can be undressed quickly.

In 1900 underclothes were not seen in public. By 1914 one might catch a glimpse of a petticoat; and between the wars briefs were frequently visible. They could be seen

on the beaches where girls changed quite openly, on the seats in the underground or buses, on the tiered seats in circuses, theatres and sports stadiums. Girls on bicycles, playing games, gathering fruit usually wore shorter skirts and were even more likely to show their briefs. On the tennis courts very short skirts became fashionable and the slightest movement revealed the underwear. The word "briefs" was so widely adopted that a group of middle-aged French writers got together to try to stop it being included in dictionaries because they felt it was being improperly substituted for the word they had used in their youth.

Observations
During the Algerian war some doc-

tors noted eye troubles among the Muslim women who had suddenly stopped wearing their veils and also taken to short European skirts.

An Indian girl wrote an article in a woman's magazine on how she had had to get used to the discomfort of wearing a suspender belt, having her legs partly bare and wearing skirts of a different length. She felt as though she were a different person.

In 1928 women suffered a less severe shock to their sensibility than the Muslim women, but it was still strong enough to mark their behaviour. The feeling of being naked under a dress was new for them, although it had been experienced by every woman from antiquity to the Second Empire, with the exception of the times when the subligaculum or drawers were worn. Throughout western history women had been aware of their bodies, particularly where their thighs brushed together, but for eighty years drawers had put a stop to that, and rediscovering nudity was disturbing. Shedding the corset which brought so much freedom, also brought apprehension. The short loose dresses of 1928 afforded more freedom of movement than any garment since the Spartan tunic, but they also caused some uneasiness. Legs were no longer protected by skirts, they were not even in contact with them very much, and women were never quite certain what their dresses would do next. In their hesitant state they alternated between extreme boldness and timidity — particularly as the looseness of cami-

knickers or knickers was no protection against surprises.

The reaction after 1928 in favour of longer, closer-fitting skirts may have been due to a sudden desire for defence. This theory seems to be supported by the manufacture of other clothes designed to calm women's anxiety.

The new outer clothes afforded more security and so did underwear. With garters stockings had been worn to just above the knee, with suspender belts they reached to mid-thigh, and it was no longer necessary to pull them up frequently and tighten them round the garters. Well-fitting briefs meant safety.

The severity of the nineteenth century dissolved after World War I and women found themselves too

Tree for Two. American illustration, 1940. <u>Below</u>: Drawing by René Giffey, 1939. <u>Below left</u>: Workshop of the Twilifit corset factory, Portsmouth, U.S.A., 1939.

Little Boy Blue

Little Boy Blue,
    Awake from your sleep;
The girl of your dreams
    Is bewitching your sheep.

How does she do it?
    That's plain to see;
It's the glamour she gets
    From her Life Bras three.

From morn, 'til night,
    At work, at play,
Be a dream girl too
    The Formfit way.

Life BY Formfit

LOOK FOR [Life] THIS LABEL
KEEP A BRA WARDROBE
Day Life— Sports Life— Night Life
$1.25—$1.75—$2.50—$3.50

FLAT CHESTED? WRITE FOR INFORMATION ABOUT INFLATION
—THE BRASSIERE FOR FLAT CHESTED WOMEN

exposed after being too restricted, so they needed to tone down the new excesses which affected their sensibilities as much as the old ones had done. The history of fashion is not only concerned with taste, but also sensibility as it affects all of those sensations experienced by the body.

Cover of the magazine *Corsets and Brassieres*, U.S.A., 1942. Below: The total comfort of elasticity, even for sport. Warner styles, U.S.A., 1937. Below left: Advertisement in *Corsets and Brassieres*, U.S.A., 1937. Far left: Advertisement, 1940s, U.S.A.

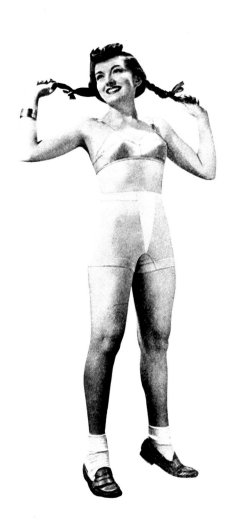

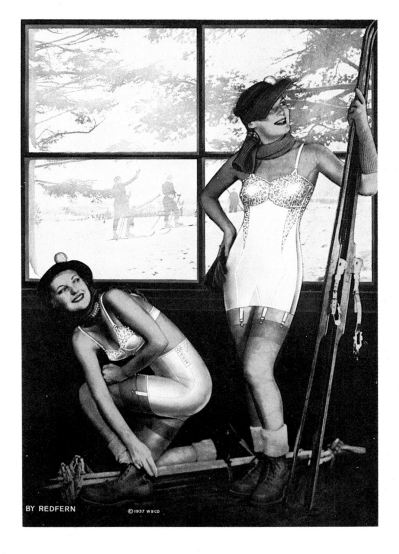

Illustrations from the brochure *Scandale*, France, 1945. This luxurious publication praising the qualities of the Scandale girdle, comprised 8 nude studies by famous artists. A transparent glossy sheet with the silhouette of a girdle was superimposed over each nude form. The nakedness was thus transparently clothed. <u>Opposite, above:</u> *Nude* by Jean Cocteau; <u>below</u>, *Nude* by Christian Bérard; <u>page right:</u> *Nude* by Benito. The Scandale girdle, made of latexed material (latex-coated thread) was one of the great success stories of the 1940s.

GETTING UP TO DATE

Immediately after World War II Europe was poor and this was reflected in underwear. Girls had lost the habit of wearing stockings, and made do with dye for their legs. Briefs became as small as the *cache-sexe* worn by striptease artistes, and black and white replaced pink as the predominant colours. Brassières became more widespread and were worn by young girls too, but nothing remained of the under-tunic – cami-knickers were dead. The scanty underwear worn by French girls after the liberation could be worn just as easily under trousers as under a skirt, and trousers became increasingly popular, particularly as some of the Vichy police, invoking the laws of the Directory, had tried to prohibit them. In addition the slogan of the new women's magazines was: "Pilfer your brother's wardrobe!" Girls could now wear the same blue jeans and roll-neck sweater, and briefs that were interchangeable with men's.

Bra and panty lines "Heloise", Girdle by Christian Dior, France in the 50s.
Left; Underwear by Balmain and by Paquin, 1949.

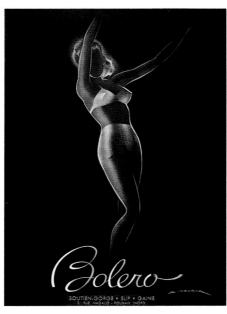

Bolero

SOUTIEN-GORGE • SLIP • GAINE
3, RUE NADAUD - ROUBAIX (NORD)

The Curve of
Fashion Favors
the Low-Cut

V-ETTE-DUET

The V-Ette Whirlpool, to
most for perfecting every
type bosom, offers a new
low-cut in answer to fashion's latest demands... adds
an extra touch of excitement
with a saucy, hip-curving
garter belt to match!

HOLLYWOOD
MAXWELL
COMPANY
6773 Hollywood Boulevard
HOLLYWOOD 28, CALIFORNIA

Girdles and Bra, France, 1947. Advertisement for Bolero, France, 1946. Advertisement V. ETTE. DUET, U.S.A., 1946. Centre: Bra for active women worn by an air-hostess, U.S.A. 1946. In France during the war, the people in charge of the women's army discussed what would be the most appropriate underwear for their recruits: lace panties or jersey briefs? They opted for the jersey briefs.

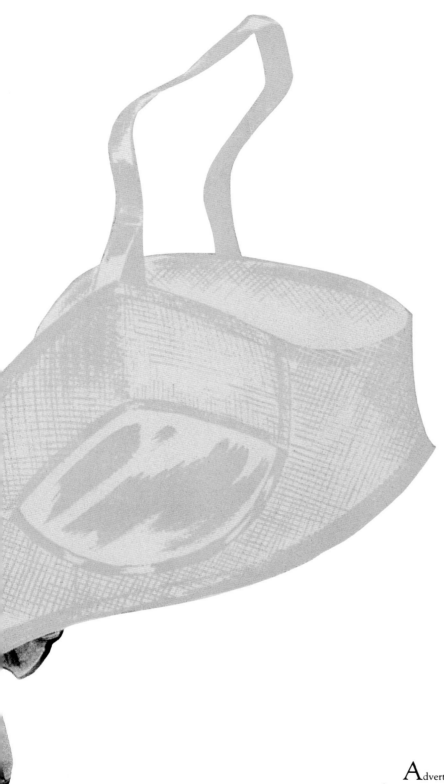

Advertisement for latex corset-making, France, 1948.
Advertisement for J. Mille & Co, France, 1946.
Advertisement for Renovex and Lady, France, 1945.

197

Black corset, 1948. Photo by Horst. Below: Model from Jacques Fath in the 40's, Photo by Robert Capa. Right: Advertisement for Highams, 1948. Photo by John French.

One new feature was that certain groups of girls started to dictate fashion, and women in their thirties went to St. Germain-des-Près to keep up-to-date. The girls there were slightly lesbian, very emancipated, tough but warm hearted, rather like Anouilh's heroines *Antigone* and *la Sauvage*. Jean-Paul Sartre also looked to them for inspiration.

After being forbidden to dance for four years, they would jive fiercely until dawn in the most dilapidated cellars they could find. Camping, youth hostelling and fresh air were out. The fashion was for hair to hang down round a pale face that never saw the sun and was bare of make-up.

In their eagerness for simplicity some of them stopped wearing briefs altogether, unless they were going to do a particularly energetic dance when they would put on a communal pair kept in the bar.

Whilst people were wondering if these girls were rebels or revolutionaries they proved that they were above all law-abiding and obedient. They immediately followed the decrees of Paris couturiers who started to dictate fashion again once prosperity returned, and to show their power, dropped skirts down to calf-length.

Women had to stay thin, but their hips had to be more rounded. Disappointed because there was no lingerie to support their creations the couturiers tried to re-introduce the petticoat. They came up against a

Petticoats and camisoles, French models, 1948: evening petticoat in pink moire (Worth); long-line (strapless) bra with matching petticoat in taffeta (Paquin); petticoat-camisole in white satin (Molyneux); petticoat in mauve silk chiffon (Jacques Heim).

At right: Voluminous briefs, French model, 1948; lawn and insertion from Valenciennes.
Far right: Nylon stocking manufacture, in the 40s. Photo by Doisneau. Nylon stockings appeared at the same time as nylon in 1938 — an idea of the Du Pont de Nemours company.

new prejudice: underwear made the figure fatter. At first women resisted all efforts to get them to wear anything like a petticoat. But film producers needed them if they wanted to have an erotic scene and not be censored, and so the audience began to think that all stars wore slips or cami-knickers.

After a rapid tussle cami-knickers, victorious after World War I, were defeated by the slip after World War II. This choice confirms something we have already observed during this hygiene-conscious age – women preferred their bodies to be in direct contact with their outer garments.

Skirts got shorter in 1953 and became more bouffant in 1958, as though trying to imitate the crinoline, but they did not change underwear. Women still wore a bra, briefs, suspender belt and a slip, or occasionally cami-knickers. Sometimes (following the alternation of composite garments and their separate parts) briefs were also suspender belts or girdles. The latter were called panty-girdles if they were closed between the legs. If they were open briefs were worn under or over them – or none were worn at all. The short girdles started from the waist, but longer ones inspired by the corset, and going up to the chest came back into fashion. They were intended to accentuate the waist and support the breasts, and were called "wasps" or corselets.

Since 1950 the wealth of very soft

Bra and girdle, Antinea, France, in the 50s.
Below: Corset by the House of Sylphide, England, 1953.
Far left: Bra in black tulle and extensible girdle, England, 1950.

Advertisement for
Scandale, Gruau. The
style of Gruau in
advertising fashion
drawings, in particular for
underwear, suddenly
outdated all that had
come before him.
Left: Advertisement
(which was never
published) for Dior
stockings, Gruau, 1953.

natural and synthetic materials, the great increase in the lingerie industry and the power of advertising have lead to a wide variety of styles, speedy changes in design and a whole galaxy of colours.

During a single season a fashionable woman would wear the newest underclothes together with some of very early origin. Under tennis shorts she would wear briefs rather like the knickers of 1930; under trousers, a panty-girdle almost to the knee, reminiscent of Renaissance drawers; little bloomers under a golf skirt; an eighteenth century petticoat under a cocktail dress; a high corset descended from the medieval corset, together with the tiny briefs of the liberation, under an evening gown. And yet further changes could be made with a foundation slip, cami-knickers, tights, leotards, and bra-slips.

This profusion of styles is available in a variety of materials, some hard-wearing, some see-through, elastic or openwork, in black, white, or depending on the year, brown, navy blue, or gold following the James Bond craze, checked, flowered, scalloped, piped or trimmed. There can never too much to choose from and now, women mix things eagerly.

Long-line (strapless) bra, Simone Perele, France, 1952. Photo by Deval.
Right: Bra with matching panties in a brown topaz colour, in crepe de Chine lined with thin batiste and latex lace, with ochre-coloured lace insertions from Alençon, French model, 1950.
Far right: Girdle with matching bra, Gossard, England, 50s.

At the beginning of the 50s, the feminine figure changes: it becomes longer and thinner, with high round breasts, and a very flat stomach. Again the corset is required to accentuate the slimmer figure and to allow close-fitting clothes to be worn. The forerunners of the new shape — wasp waist, curvaceous breasts and hips — are Marcel Rochas who invented the "waspie" in 1945, and Dior who imposes his "New Look" in 1947.

Chantal

Caroline

SOUTIEN-GORGE
GAINES LINGERIE
JEKOSS
la ligne jeune

SCANDALE

STAR
SOUTIEN-GORGE

Centre, at left:
Dress in black woollen
material by Patou and
girdle in nylon tulle by
Lefaucheur — Patou
(worn by the models
presenting the collection
for Winter 1953).
At right: Dress in black
velvet by Dior and all-in-
one corselette in black
latex tulle by Lefaucheur-
Dior.
Vignettes: Advertisements
by French corset-makers
in the 50s.

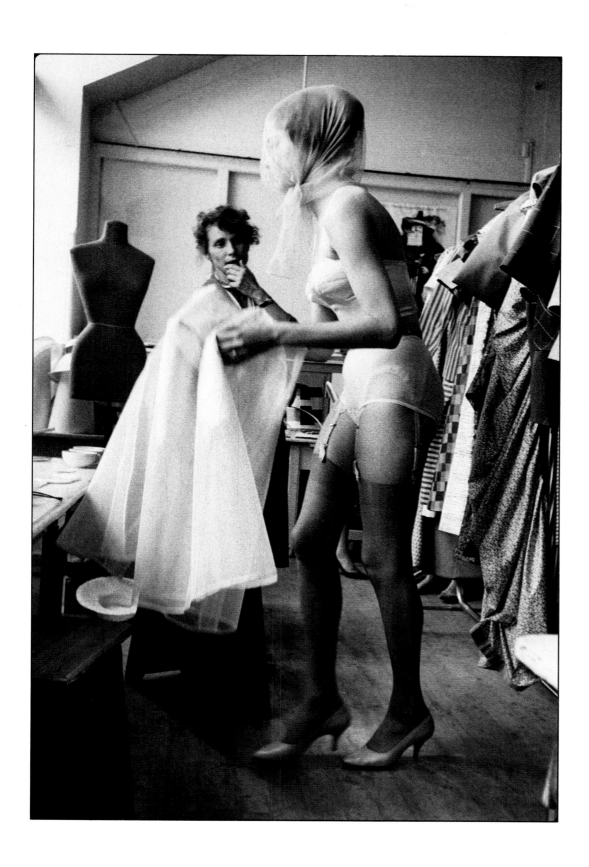

A model changing her clothes during a fashion show organized by the Stedelijk Museum, Amsterdam, in the 50s. Photo by Leonard Freed.
Below: Body-bra with suspender belt in white nylon lace, strapless but with lace cups that separate the breasts: it can be worn over an elastic girdle (under an afternoon dress or a two piece suit), by Balenciaga-Lefaucheur, France, 1954.
Left: Advertising campaign by the French Silk Commission, 1956.
Next two pages: Dancers from the Crazy Horse, Paris, in the 50s. Photos by Paul de Cordon.

Gina Lollobrigida, *Anna de Brooklyn*, 1958. The short filmsy transparent nightie in uncrushable nylon radically revolutionizes night wear. It was imported from the U.S. and created by Nancy Melcher.
Below: Martine Caroll in the 50s.

Joan Collins, *Rally round the Flag Boys*, 1959. *Les Orgueilleux*, Michelle Morgan.
<u>Below</u>: Marilyn Monroe in a negligee.
<u>Below</u>: *Cat on a Hot Tin Roof*. Liz Taylor. In the 50s, moviemakers used the camisole-slip often. It was a trick to reveal part of the body without infringing the censorship laws. But female moviegoers, without being aware of the mysteries of the movie industry, will soon adopt this demure style as an accessory indispensable for seduction. The camisole-slip was again in fashion.

Although the popularity of the camisole-slip is growing rapidly due to the influence of the stars, the petticoat is more characteristic of the trend in the 50s. The petticoat widens skirts to a bell-shape accentuating the slimness of the waist and the shape of the bust which is now the "hot" part of the body in fashion.

<u>Below</u>: *The Parisian*, Brigitte Bardot.
<u>Right</u>: Skirts and petticoats in the style of the 50s, Germany, 1985. Photo by Susan Lemer.

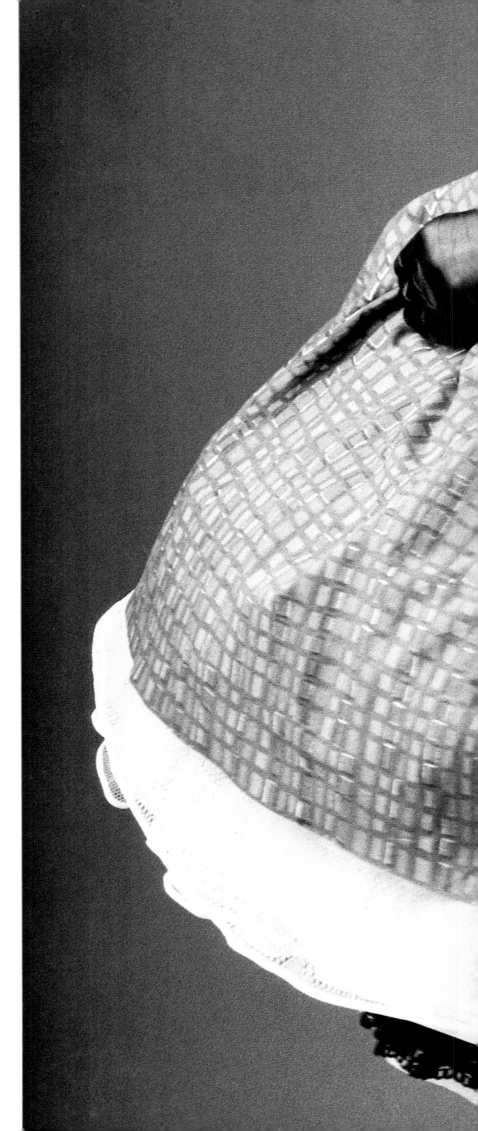

Long-line bra with "peplum" by Rochas, France, 1952. Photo by Seeberger.
Below: A dancer, France 1957.
Far left: "The Merry Widow", Warner, U.S.A., 1952; This long-line bra in white or black acetate was one of Warner's great successes.

219

Night dress, Vanity Fair, 1966; photo by Lionel Kazan; in run-resistant nylon, with a scooped neckline front and back, adorned with a large flounce at the bottom and gathers under the breasts tightened with a side fastening.
Right: Bra with matching panties by Warner, 1965. Photo by J.J. Bugat; in lycra tulle with pastel flowers (a matching girdle available).

Two different types of bra created by Frederick of Hollywood or, the courtesans' "battle dress" within every woman's grasp, U.S.A., in the 60s.
Below: The "Stechbra", Warner, U.S.A., 1963; this bra is a real innovation: except for the cups, it is entirely elastic. What is most revolutionary are the extendable straps which until then, were made of non-elastic material. The straps can be moved on the shoulder according to the neckline but they will not slip off the shoulder. This style will be imitated by many manufacturers.

Right: Black corset, U.S.A., 1962. Photo by Jeanloup Sieff.
Following pages, left: Ban-Lon underwear, France, 1967; right: "Panty stockings", Tout-Dim in elasticized nylon, France, 1967. Tights will only appear in 1958 and commercialized at the beginning of the 60s.

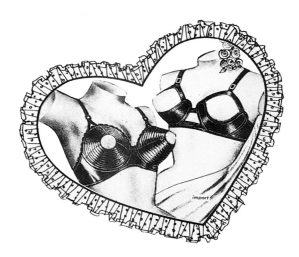

THE LATEST FASHIONS:
1 9 6 5 – 1 9 8 5

Consumer society reached its highest point in the mid-1960s. Capitalism was in an optimistic mood and believed that femininity, like the car, contributed to social order and prosperity. The Church raised no objection. In France the government repressed erotic literature and one could land in front of the magistrates merely by reprinting the works of de Sade, but the exuberance of female undergarments was regarded as the peak of creative art, free of any "sinful" connotations. Photos of lightly clad women, which before the war would have been restricted to saucy magazines, now featured openly in advertisements and in the fashion pages. Prima donnas and film stars were only too willing to show how they looked in suspenders, how they slipped into a petticoat or cami-knicker.

When in the thirteenth century Louis IX had allowed undergarment makers to display what they had sewn during the night, near the cemetery of the Innocents, the results of their labours remained a secret ten leagues beyond Paris; and if during the Re-

Rosy-Doll in blue nylon lace, cup with removable cup frames, Rosy, France, 1967.
Left: Lange, Berlin, 1979. Photo by Helmut Newton.

Pantie-girdle in
lycra and lurex, by
Warner, 1966. Photo by
Lionel Kazan.
Below: Dress by Louis
Feraud, Ergee stockings,
France, in the 60s. As
skirts become shorter, it is
necessary to wear, if not
full tights, at least
stockings that stop half-
way up the thigh and are
self-suppporting. The
suspender belt disappears.
The suspenders are
cleverly concealed inside
the pantie-girdle.
Far right: Tights in
embroidered lace, by
Cadolle, France, in the
60s, lace by Tiburce
(Calais), elastified by
Sarlane (so that the tights
will not wrinkle).

naissance, Catherine de Médicis and her ladies-in-waiting wore drawers, ordinary French women as a whole knew nothing of it; and even as late as the German occupation a number of French peasant women were unaware of the existence of knickers. But by 1965 the underwear industry had gained access to a massive distribution system and its slightest whim became the ruling fashion. The

new trend foreshadowed by the appearance of panties. The outcome was still the same: it protected the woman by imprisoning her in a kind of chastity belt.

Meanwhile, slacks were multiplying at the expense of dresses and skirts. This looked as though the long evolution, which restricted man while leaving woman more flexible, had suddenly become exhausted and

Window of a Parisian shop in the 60s. Photo by P. Borel. *Below:* The *jupant*, by Corjoli, 1967; it is a combination of the panty-girdle with a close-fitting petticoat. *Left:* Panties with matching bra, Kayser, France, in the 60s; lace by Tiburce Lebas (Calais), elastified by Sarlane. *Following pages, left:* Stretch stockings, panties with matching bras, created by Succès, Le Printemps department store, France, 1967; Photo by Sacha; they are in lycra available in nine colors. *Right:* Panty with removable suspenders, Formit, France, in the 60s; in lycra, with a scooped back designed especially for wearing low-waist trousers or skirts; available in white and in "powder-cloud"

working class, now adopting middle class standards, was all the more impressed, in that, like cars and kitchen gadgets, underwear had become a sign of social advancement.

Only very young girls could display originality which, while this did not give rise to new fashion, at least modified existing trends. Having decided to wear suspenders over their knickers, they did not bring about a change in the design of mass-produced garments, but confirmed a

that a unisex style based on male fashions was taking over. This view gained wide acceptance because the mood of the day favoured the equality of the sexes, the equality of fashion, even the equality of examination results, and student power was only too ready to sweep away the festoonings of lace which the reign of the Pill had made absurd. In the United States the protesters were jettisoning and burning their bras.

A few years had been sufficient to

transform the furbelows and flounces, which had been the very symbols of post-war prosperity into quaint museum pieces. Now uniformly dressed in jeans and T-shirts they could easily have swapped with men, women could only tolerate as underwear, tights, slips, bras which were strictly utilitarian.

The years 1965 – 1970 witnessed a revolution in tastes. When women opted for pantyhose or panties, short or Bermuda length — they were covering their lower limbs, the area of their thighs which had traditionally been left bare. When an advertisement for pantyhose proclaimed "suspenders are out of date", it unknowingly championed the constriction of the body. Stretch panties, like corsets of old, laid claim to an orthopedic role: they flatten your stomach — wear them and you will lose three kilos! Indeed by now undergarments were no longer mysterious, but austere and practical, while under the label of "fun", underwear was downgraded by the use of patterns designed for overgarments — from tartan to Indian designs. Bold and bright, they relegated to the past, which now seemed increasingly remote, all the old diaphanous and lustrous fabrics. A mere couple of years had been enough to put an end to the frivolity with which women had celebrated the end of wartime austerity. In line with unisex T-shirts and jeans, women believed that they only wanted undergarments which

were sober, functional, simple in design and made with synthetic fabrics which needed no ironing, were easily and quickly washed, and fitted any shape. A 19th-century lady would not have been too surprised probably by the fashions of the mid-1960's. She would have recognised in the girdles, the cami-knickers, the bras, the suspenders, her own corset split into

mained. Fashion writers even began to ignore them altogether. Stockings which had no need of suspenders came on the scene; rising well up the thigh, they claimed to fit in with the mini style, to be finer than hose and in certain cases to "adapt perfectly to your measurements", thanks to an adjustable flat buckle. However, like Dior's thigh girls, they had the draw-

à robe sage (ou folle),... il faut Mitoufle
le vrai Mitoufle

à robe courte,...il faut Mitoufle
le vrai Mitoufle !

separate parts. But after 1966, on the other hand, she could easily have gained the impression that fashion had been transformed by an invasion or an earthquake!

Suspenders did survive, but the sudden appearance of the miniskirt forced them to beat a hasty strategic retreat. They were compelled to become very short in an effort to hide behind what skirt or dress still re-

back of running counter to the contemporary trend: they left the upper thigh bare, instead of hermetically enclosing the body.

On the grounds of efficiency, metal was added to swimwear and the "waist-tight petticoat" was devised — a short-lived form of torture. For less formal occasions one finds bermuda-length pyjamas in some competition with short-sleeve shirts and shorty-

Body-Dim, Dim, France, 1970; 40-denier stretch bodystocking (20-denier for the legs), close-fitting like tights, with shaped breast and thin elastic straps; colours: natural, *palma* (pale caramel), earth, black. At the end of the 60s, underwear tends to be more natural and to evoke nudity. The all-in-one bodystocking nourishes illusions.
<u>Right</u>: Net stockings, France, 1976.

nighties, brief but modest, in naive flowery patterns. Breasts were required to be completely juvenile.

During this period the reduction of underwear to a strictly functional role had been fiercely supported by feminists who, loathing the woman-as-sex-object idea, thought themselves powerful enough to replace her with the sexless woman. The protracted struggle of the years 1966–1986 often gave the impression that they were gaining the upper hand, but victory is often illusory and one detail can change everything.

Let us take one example: the body stocking, an undergarment which was claimed "to shape your legs, fit neatly around the hips, give an impeccable shape to your waist and make your bosom more beautiful by adapting itself to your every movement, a creation which adds to your beauty and your freedom". Such a development could be interpreted as the success of a campaign aimed at the chaste reclusion of woman. But under this supple and light material, women, it turned out, felt disconcertingly naked and were affected by this sensation, heightened by the emergence of the maxi, (whether *haute couture* or improvised) whose excesses soon matched those of the mini.

It is hardly surprising that the mini-skirt should have caused such turmoil in underwear fashions, because by uncovering the legs it disrupted a code of modesty which went back centuries. One has to go back to

236

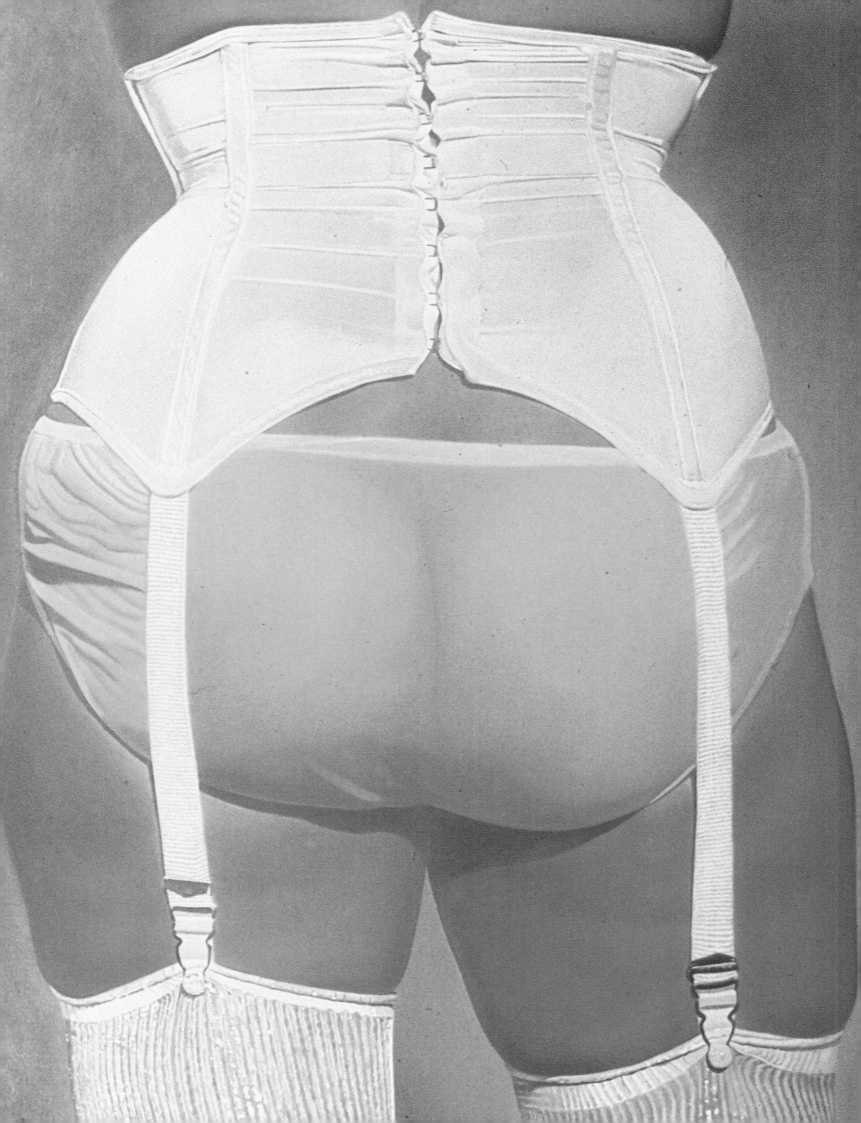

those girls whom Spartans called phaïnomerides, *"those who display their thighs"*, to find such boldness. Admittedly, if one remembers that sportswear often tends to become townwear, tennis shorts which pre-date the Second World War should have helped us foresee such a revolution. But it had progressed at lightning speed, whereas previously changes in fashion had always gone through slow transitional stages. Shorts had certainly accustomed women to reveal important areas of their bodies, but they had a protective element which skirts lacked. The triumph of the miniskirt, which caused mothers to dress like their daughters and their daughters like little girls, was not only a student-like glorification of youth, but also of femininity, and it helped to hold in check the masculinization of clothes. This, although promoted both by jeans manufacturers and by *haute couture*, was undermined by a multitude of details which proved that women had not decided to adopt uniformity: high heels worn with a trouser suit, at first a sign of the worst taste, became indispensable, and loosely tied cravats were not so much a symbol of bohemianism as the correct accessory for a stylish young woman. Whereupon the maxiskirt appeared with the same rapidity, the same lack of transition. Fashion had developed a new dynamism, enabling it to swing from one extreme to another and thus deal another blow

to the unisexist Utopia. The body was being rediscovered inside long, floating dresses (reminiscent of a distant past), which possessed a protective value that allowed undergarments to be totally eliminated rather than multiplied. The skin replaced the body stocking, breasts enjoyed a freedom which, thanks to transparent fabrics, they could display.

Dress designers followed rather than led. The first maxis were worn by hippies whose skirts trailed in the dust from Los Angèles to Katmandu to Place Saint-Michel. Meanwhile Yves Saint-Laurent was holding firm to his belief in the victory of the androgynous style, but, carried away by an irresistible storm, he was forced to change direction and moved into the hyper-sexual. He maintained that his creations were influenced by

Summer underwear, France, 1971, drawings by Philippe Castle; *from left to right*: bra and panties in thin white Dropnyl Helanca net (Peter Pan); two-piece, leotard-style, in yellow and navy blue striped Helanca (Habella); two "landscape" brassieres in Enka Glanzstoff crepe with insertions of boats, waves and clouds (by Emmanuelle Khan for Eris) with matching stockings (Le Bourgets). Left: Gretchen, John Kacere, 1970.

DIM.

Les collants Dim commencent à 3 F.
Collant Classique 3 F.
Collant Longues Jambes 4 F.
Collant Jour 5 F.
Collant Opaque 6 F.
Collant Soleil 6,50 F.
Collant Transparent 7,50 F.

American pop artists but in the same interview, even though he denied having given in to Pigalle eroticism, claimed he had followed "people" who, after wanting "to seek refuge in the anonymity of a uniform" now wished to enter the limelight. "Young men want to grow beards and girls want to express their deep sense of femininity", he said. He thought he was responding to a passing whim, while any historian of western style would have regarded the reaction as inevitable.

In the very year (1971) when fashion writers were polishing off their last obituaries of the mini, women rediscovered it in the wardrobe and began wearing it again. Maxi, midi, mini — the three ways of asserting one's womanhood.

By 1972 one could be justified in believing that the fashion world had been shaken by more storms in just a few years than had occurred during the whole half-century, but through all these changes one trend remained constant: the rejection of any move to abolish the sexual symbolism of clothes. Even during the short reign of the unisex style, women had persisted in affirming their difference by the use of a range of accessories. Nevertheless, their concern was restricted to external appearances and one magazine, which devoted a section of one of its 1972 issues to a review of the previous ten years, did not make one reference to underwear.

And yet underground they sur-

A model from Nina Ricci being offered a spray of flowers to celebrate her ten years employment with Nina Ricci, France, in the 70s. Photo by Eve Arnold. <u>Left</u>: C. Dior, Paris, 1977. Photo by Helmut Newton.

vived, marginal and clandestine; Dior had remained faithful to them during this crossing of the desert. A few American firms had specialised in provocative products which European women could buy from mail order catalogues. Magazines such as *Playboy* and *Lui* displayed women in suggestive clothing, the film world did the same; but this anachronism can be explained by a nostalgia of the

ders. It was a good sign.

I had no doubt that women would not habitually refuse to distinguish themselves from men by their undergarments, but I nevertheless heaved a sigh of relief when a few suspenders made their appearance in 1977 fashion magazines. These photographs were included with some reluctance and bore captions like: "Since they seem to like them …"

imagination called Retro style. I knew women who had not surrendered, but to find a pair of stockings, they had to make special efforts which showed how few these remaining devotees of the cult really were. And yet, one evening at Castel's, as I was lamenting the decline of lingerie, three of my fellow guests, an actress, a novelist, and a member of Dior's staff, proved to me that they all, demonstrably, were wearing suspen-

But opinion polls soon confirmed that both men and women were in favour of them — and not only aged cranks or old maids, but men in their thirties and young girls. A very proper daily paper devoted a two-page spread to the resurrection of underwear, whilst tights, now on the defensive, took to seams designed to arouse idle speculation. Simultaneously skirts and dresses — whose demise some people had already celebrated — were overtaking trousers.

In 1976, Sabbia Rosa alone, had displayed in a shop miraculously situated in front of the *Librarie des Femmes*, examples of high quality lingerie which seemed no more than a memory — or a faint hope. Five years later, they were on show in department stores. And in 1985 a firm as specialised in mass marketing as the *Trois Suisses*, published a catalogue exclusively devoted to lingerie for the first time.

It marked the rehabilitation of fine materials (silk, cotton), of lace and diaphanous fabrics, flouncy knickers contrasting with the plainness of panties. Strapless and half-cup bras, back from limbo, regained favour, at times appearing as part of a dress style in their own right, just like the sleeve vest which turned into a bodice, or the camisole and broderie anglaise knickers. But underwear remains underwear, it has regained its status. A poster appeared on Paris buildings showing a woman, thighs encased in nylons, held over a man's shoulder with the slogan: "The tights that carry you away". Manufacturers abandoned the idea of praising the practical qualities of tights, trying instead to open up a fantasy world to the consumer — a stratagem designed to fail. Tights are neuter.

On the beaches, clinging swimsuits are cut away above the thigh line, requiring some degree of depilation; close by, string costumes hide almost nothing in front and nothing at all

from the back. There is another style of dress: total nudity, which had long left behind the candour of the early naturists. These are the three ways of dealing both with one's body and with the admiration of others. They are not contradictory.

Such co-existence is typical of our time. Just as those three styles of beachwear form a coherent pattern, so do the mini, the flouncy maxi, slacks, shorts, skirts which reached down to calf level, or others which stop at the knee. All these are part of fashion. And hair can be worn long or short, flowing loosely or in a short symmetrical cut. Ecumenism reigns, and for the first time in history women are freed from strict dress rules.

Awareness of underwear is another significant aspect. In 1978 I wrote: "Twenty years ago women wore suspender belts under their skirts quite

Around 1975, refined underwear and luxurious fabrics reappeared, a trend led by the small craftsmen, who were mostly young women in their thirties. They unanimously declared that they were weary of the prevailing unisex and sterile fashions. But the general public was not yet ready for this new "post-feminist" look and it will take some time: in 1982, 54 percent of women declared that they never wore elegant underwear; 10 percent declared that they often wore elegant underwear; while 23 percent said that they sometimes wore it. (French survey conducted by the "Club Expansion Lingerie"). "Waspie" in white Swiss cotton muslin trimmed with small bows, with matching bikini panties (Pascale Madonna), white stockings (Gerbe); France; 1985. Photo by Steve Hiett.
Right: Panties, bra and suspender belt in silk, by La Perla, Italy 1985. Photo by Tony Thorimbert.

innocently and quite naturally. Today they are aware that this deliberate act has a meaning — for them and for others. And that is new" When I was sketching out this semantic change in contemporary underclothes, it was indeed new, but since then it has become manifest from Canada to Japan, from the United States to Greece. My 1978 audience consisted essentially of initiates, but now Carlo Castellaneta can be understood by a wide public when he writes in *Etichetta* that men ought to erect a statue to the inventor of the suspender belt, adding: "Its use is not as widespread as when it merely served to hold stockings up, but a woman who buys one today does so with erotic intent". Some don the suspender belt only for an evening from which they expect certain emotional events; others even go as far as putting them on just to go to bed. In short, it belongs to the *woman-as-woman*, a new term which replaces that of *woman-as-sex-object*, a phrase earnest activists of the "feminist" movement still desperately cling to as they try to banish every shred of charm from advertising.

Many women, some because they are still influenced by the idealogy of desexualisation, resist the sensual, textural interplay of intimate seductiveness. They are bitter towards men who admit being so attracted, and even more so towards their sisters who stand accused of putting on

"fripperies" to accommodate the fantasies of neurotics. This peevishness brings a serene smile to the lips of those sinners who know that to bewitch so as to become bewitched, is one of the greatest pleasures.

The evolution of dress styles follows too few laws for one to be able to predict its future direction. The Comte de Vaublanc recalls in his *Memoirs* that shortly before the French Revolution, he had met, in a disused wing of his college, an old monk who believed that God had ordered him in anticipation of a new Flood, to discover animal and vegetable forms that bore no resemblance to those of Nature, so that life could begin again from zero. The monk was suffering a real martyrdom, wielding his charcoal pencil along blackened walls; for as soon as he thought he had made a breakthrough he discovered that he had merely merged two

Waspie in beige silk satin with matching panties (Sabbia Rosa), stockings (DD), France, 1985. Photo by Mike Yavel.
Left: Seura-Bernard outfit, France, 1980. Photo by Jean-Robert Franco.

U nderwired bra, rolled double straps, panties with high-cut legs, Warner, France, 1986; the outfit is also available with a bra without underwires, fancy panties, buttonned briefs, all in white.

Right: Bra without underwires, thin straps "tanga" panties with matching garter belt, Warner, France, 1986. Also available with a chemisette, Retro-fashion briefs and underwired bras.

From Goldie Lingerie, France, 1984. Photo by Catherine Panchout; high briefs buttoned in the back, "old fashioned" bra in cotton printed with roses on a coral or grey background, with a matching towelling peignoir.
Right: Underwear by Eres, shirt by Charvet, France, 1984. Photo by Paul Lange; bra and bikini panties in cotton knit printed with small hearts; colours: pink and blue.

unrelated forms combining the two kingdoms in a meaningless mixup.

Today any hope of discovering new clothes is equally pointless — especially undergarments which, more closely associated with the body, are more subject to the demands of its architecture. Admittedly, for centuries various solutions have been designed to ensure that a fabric can be tight enough to hold to the body yet loose enough to be discarded if required. A contradiction overcome by draping, by using strips of material, by tying the ends of a piece of cloth or adjusting it by a range of fixtures such as buckles, laces, pins, buttons, studs, hooks, fasteners, zips — more recently elastic or adhesive material. And if in years to come a new technology does bring about new methods of opening and closing, it would be unrealistic to expect totally new forms to emerge.

On the other hand one can predict that fashion will remain dependent on its own inherent and constant dynamics. It is equally likely that the co-existence of differing garments will continue to allow women to alter according to the day or the hour, their style, the way they look and the way they feel. At the risk of being proved wrong I will hazard the guess that the somewhat perverse relationships of past and present, of

daywear and nightwear, of clothes and underclothes, will be more accentuated.

A few years ago the underbodice and the drawers of the early part of this century were rediscovered for both sleeping and waking hours; similarly grandmother's petticoats reappeared in the guise of skirts. Why then not suppose that beribboned knickers may become part of beach-wear and replace holiday shorts? Why should not undergarments find new ways of revealing themselves as decorated pantalettes which might peep from beneath skirts like those of the little girls of Victorian days?

For fifteen years we have witnessed a struggle between a profusion of flounces and an almost Spartan severity which triumphed only to be defeated in the end, but nothing allows us to conclude that the wheel will not turn once more, a revolution which would be no more final than all the others.

Greeks still wear skirts (an ethnic dress, to be sure) and Scotsmen wear kilts; in Saint Tropez and in several Club Meds one comes across men who, with their flowing jellabas, have adopted the open style; a few coutur-iers have offered feminine solutions to the male look. This is more a disguise than a costume and the aim is less to establish a fashion than to create an effect. Similarly women who wear men's shirts and men's underpants know that they are play-ing a game. They are dressing up like a particular actress who once used to

R ibbed cotton underpants for men, La Samaritaine, France, 1985. Photo by Peter Lindberg.
<u>Far left</u>: Bra and panties in natural-coloured silk damask, Huit, France, 1985. Photo by Arthur Elgort.

Briefs by Andrea Templer, bodysuit by Agnes B, France, 1985. Photo by Eddy Kohli. Nowadays there is a wide selection of swimming costumes: the bikini (still very popular), the one-piece suit (in the 30s style or with super high-cut legs if it is influenced by the jumpsuit), the topless (whose forerunner was the monokini with straps), the 'tanga' also called 'enrolados' (from Brazil: it varies between the classical one-piece suit and the topless with super-high rolled legs), the G-string (that reveals the buttocks).
Below: Nightgown in silk satin (Apostrophes) and leotards in silk tightened at the waist (Chantal Thomass), France, 1985. Photo by Oliviero Toscani.
Right: Mini jacket (in pink or black gingham) on top of a nylon push-up bra worn with a waist-high, front-opening skirt, by Jean-Paul Gaultier, France, 1985. Photo by Eddy Kohli. The trend is to design underwear as a complementary part of clothes — in fact, to match them.
Following pages: Underwear by Chantal Thomass, France, 1985. Photo by Christian Moser.

play the part of Napoleon's son. In the same way, in the eighteenth century, the Tsars, or rather the Tsarinas, used to plan balls at which women were dressed as men and men as women, without anyone being taken in by the masquerade.

Underwear, because it clings to those parts of the female body which are the most secret, the most exciting and, for man, the most dramatic, does not belong exclusively to the world of fashion. It is dominated by the imagination, and women move into dangerous territory if they forget that it is above all an incomparable weapon. Incomparable because its raison d'être is to please the one whose senses it delights by arousing in him the desire to reciprocate.

Spotted undergarment in damask silk: two-tone brassiere with buttoned panties (by Pascale Madonna), striped jacket (Synonyme de Georges Rech), France, 1986. Photo by Francois Pomepvi.
Far left: Undergarment in elastic lace (by Barbara) and spotted jacket (Synonyme de Georges Rech), France, 1986. Photo by Francois Pomepvi.

Italy, 1986. Photo
by Jean-Francois Lepage.
Right: Japan, 1982.
Photo by Inakoshi;
Following pages, first
double page at left:
Advertisement by
Cacharel, France, 1984.
Photo by Sarah Moon; at
right: France, 1984;
Photo by Jeanloup Sieff;
second double page:
advertisement by
Scandale, France 1986.

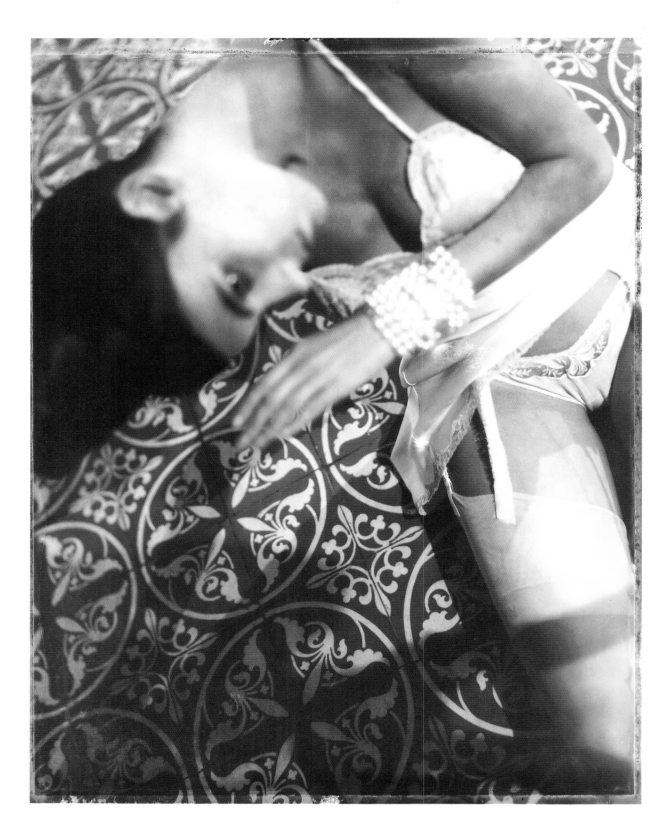

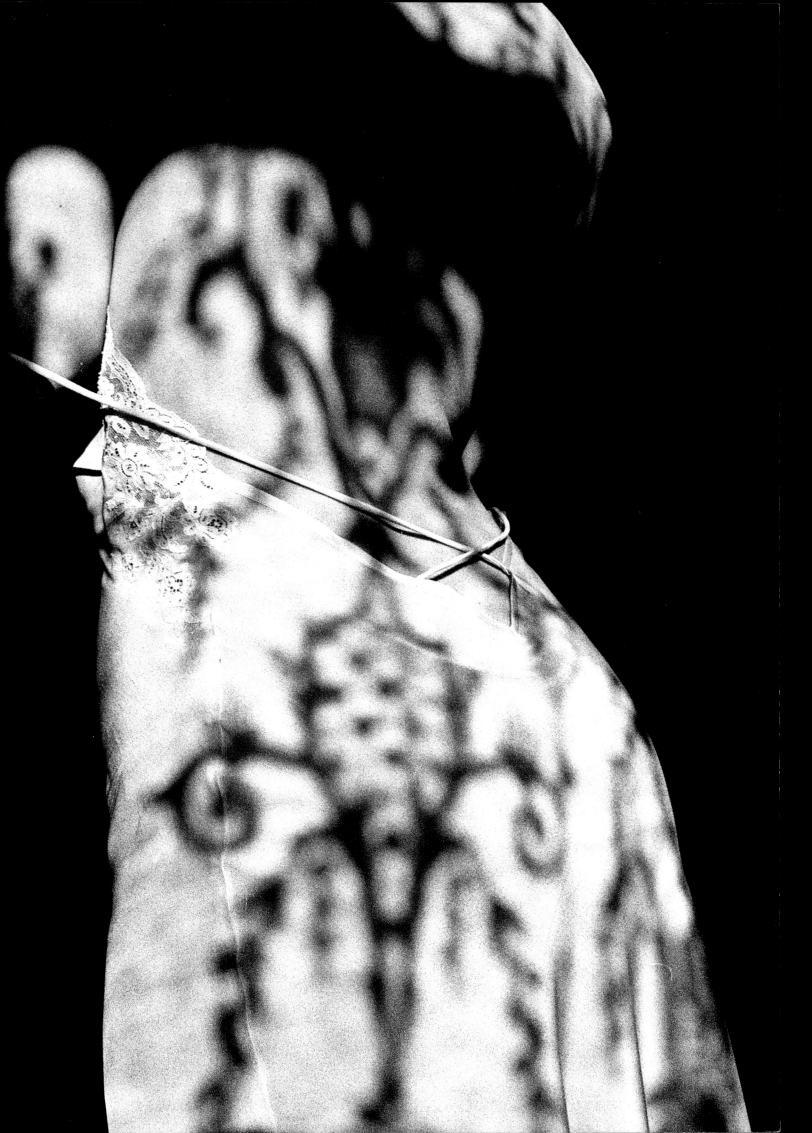

Baby Doll or nightie - Very short nightie, very often made of transparent nylon, that appeared late in the 50s after the 1956 movie, *Baby Doll* directed by Elia Kazan.

Bikini - See also Swimsuit. In July 1946, a French designer dared include in his collection a very brief two-piece swimsuit reduced to the bare minimum. Because of its "explosive" look, he named it "Bikini" after the name of the atoll where the first nuclear bomb test was conducted four days before. The original model was made of cotton printed with press clippings to emphasise its topicality.

Bikini panties - See Panties

Bloomer - Drawers worn by women, created in the middle of the 19th century by an American woman, Mrs Amelia Bloomer who tried vainly to introduce it into France and England. The word re-appeared in 1945 to describe loose voluminous panties which matching dresses worn by young girls.

Bra - The bra appeared simultaneously with the corset in 1900. Originally the corset was quite straight and low on the breasts so that it did not support them well. Small brassieres with feather shafts and breast-supports were used. That was the prelude to the introduction of the bra which will become popular in the 20s.

Busk - Thin strip of wood, whalebone or steel used for stiffening corsets. In the 16th century the busk was independent, and slid into a sheath (called the *bus-*

quière) sewn on the whalebone bodice. In the 17th century the *busquière* was concealed with embroidery. Trimmed with embroideries, or ornamental designs, the busk became an attractive accessory very much like the fan that appeared later. One century later the busk was built into the corset and was not removable. Until 1830, it consisted of one piece only, except when front laced corsets had two thin stiffening busks tied up with eyelets. In 1829. the two-piece busk appeared together with metal eyelets (1828) and new hooks that improved the lacing and unlacing of corsets. The one-piece busk stiffened by two steel strips, with eyelets or hooks on one side and buttons or clips on the other, was very popular right up until today.

Bustle - Boned demi-pannier which replaced the crinoline around 1867. It was worn under petticoats in the small of the back to push out the skirt at the back and to be used as a support for the "pouf" (voluminous drape formed by the back part of the skirt). At the end of that century, the bustle is replaced by a small cushion (called the *cul*) attached to the waist. It completely disappeared in 1899 when skirts straight on the hips appeared.

Chemise (Undershirt) - Originally this intimate undergarment was made of fine or not so fine cotton with a T-shape and long sleeves. In the second half of the 15th century, as necklines dipped, the undershirt was more visible, and trimmed with embroidery, became more sophisticated. Until the end of 19th century the shape and the trimmings changed but the material used remained the same — white linen, until later when silk and colourful materials started to be used. It was only in the 20s that the undershirt worn under corsets and petticoats disappeared. Then women began to wear corsets and other accessories right next to the skin.

Combination - One-piece undergarment combining undershirt and drawers (1892), drawers and petticoat (1897), undershirt with drawers and petticoat (1898). In the 20s the undershirt combined with drawers was an essential part of underwear. The

"combination" in the present meaning of the word, is an adaptation of the undershirt — petticoat formula, adopted in the 30's. It will be widely used until the 40s.

Corset - In the 17th and 18th centuries, the corset was designed in contrast with whalebone bodice, because it had fewer bones and therefore was not as close-fitting. Late in the 18th century, it progressively replaced the whalebone bodice before being abandoned with the introduction of neo-classical fashion. Still it re-appeared in 1804 in a shorter and lighter version, totally different from the former bodice. It did not compress the bust in a rigid cone anymore, but enhanced the slimness of the waist, supporting the breasts and concealing any flaws in the figure. In the first third of the 19th century, corset makers improved the lacing and unlacing of the corset which used to require the help of a third party. The so-called "lazy" lacing-up (1843), which later will be improved further, meant that women could lace and unlace their corset themselves. Late in the 19th century, the corset was still short on the hips and curved on the abdomen. Its shape dramatically changed in 1900 when the corset became longer and straight in the front. This shape consequently arched the back excessively and the busk was not so tight on the stomach. The overall figure was accordingly shaped like an S. Soon afterwards the corset split in two with the progressive introduction of the bra. Around 1910, with the influence of designer Poiret, the corset was more or less abandoned and will be less and less used all through the 20s. But in 1930, women again returned to their corset maker. The traditional corset had disappeared to be replaced by a kind of belt called a girdle that supported the body from the waist down to the upper part of thighs. Girdles will become less rigid over the years as elastic materials are used to make a lightweight undergarment. In the 50s the use of the "waspie" indicated a temporary return of the corset and of close-fitting undergarments.

Corset cover - Undergarment worn on top of the corset and covering the bust.

Criardes - See Pannier

Crinoline - Originally it was a coarse horsehair fabric (horsehair is translated as *crins* in French) used in 1842 for petticoats to enormously widen skirts. Around 1850 those crinoline petticoats were replaced by starched, boned petticoats, which, around 1855 were replaced by panniers consisting of a series of light steel hoops. Around 1865, steel was replaced by whalebones, hoops become oval and were used only for the lower section of the skirt which became much fuller in the back. By extension, crinoline also came to mean the hoop skirt itself.

Cul - See Bustle.

Drawers (underpants) - These most intimate of garments, which at the beginning was simply underpants made of linen or silk, were very seldom referred to or shown until the 19th century, which proves that they were not very popular. Drawers became more widely used in the 16th century but they were mostly reserved for the elite or for courtesans. The moral code condemned drawers because they were too reminiscent of the masculine role. They became more sophisticated (trimmed with lace and embroidery) at the beginning of the 19th century when women took to drawers as they copied the fashions of small children. But it was too early and it triggered off severe criticism because the drawers extended down to the ankles and were not completely concealed by the skirt. In the middle of the 19th century criticism faded and drawers were considered just another feminine accessory. Drawers, were long until 1870, shortened until 1914, when they were reduced to small straight panties. Early in the 30s the word "panties" very often replaced the word "underpants" in women's magazines.

Dressing gown - It was only in the 19th century that the dressing gown became "déshabillé" for women. Until then, and in particular in the 17th century, it was considered as a gown different from the court gown and it was worn informally in some rooms of the royal suites. At that time the dressing gown was a "déshabillé" reserved for men.

Farthingale - Originally this was a stiffened bell-shaped petticoat made even more rigid by narrow wooden battens and thick wire. It was used for widening women's skirts ungathered at the hips. It was fashionable in Spain in the 15th century and it appeared in France in the 16th century. French fashion replaced that petticoat by a circular rolled belt that distributed the gathers of a skirt all around the body. Late in the 16th century a third type of farthingale appeared shaped like a wheel or a flat drum on which the skirt opened. It was generally trimmed with a gathered frill.

Garters - Linen band passing round the leg to keep up the stocking. In the Middle Ages garters are used to support men's knee breeches. They are passed round the leg below the knee then crossed under the back and pulled tight above the knee. Later on garters became attractive accessories for women as well as for men: they were trimmed with silver or gold tags, with jewels and embroideries. In the 16th century, as machine knit woollen stockings became widely used, garters with fastenings or slipknots were quite popular. Sophisticated garters did not change much until the beginning of the 19th century when elastic started to be used. Experts first tried to use a spiralling copper wire embedded into the material itself. Then in 1832 rubber was used. But garters will not improve much until 1842 when galvanization was developed. In 1900 the garter is supplanted by the suspender (with rubber bands) attached to the corset, which was becoming more and more popular. The garter came back in fashion in the 20s when stockings rolled half-way on the thigh appeared.

Girdle - See Corset.

G-string - A "*cache-sexe*" which, at the back, is a single thin string attached to an elastic strip around the waist. It is usually worn by strippers and is occasionally used nowadays as underwear or swimwear.

Hoop-petticoat - An 18th century English term used to designate panniers.

Kimono - A wide-sleeved robe with a belt, characteristic of Japanese costume worn by both men and women. In 1920 a craze for all things Oriental brought the kimono into the wardrobe of western women. Just like house pyjamas, it became a new version of the negligee.

Knee Breeches - See Stockings

Leotard - Close-fitting one-piece garment covering the trunk of the body. It can be more or less tight-fitting, in light or mesh fabric. Nowadays leotards are worn under a skirt or under pants and are used as underwear for the lower part of the body and as a garment for the upper part. In both cases leotards bave buttons or press studs at the crotch which makes them very convenient. They can be worn directly on the skin or over a full body stocking and they are part of the wardrobes of dancers and sportswomen. Occasionally they are worn at home or as leisure wear.

Linge - A fine fabric woven from flax, silk or cotton yarns, from nylon or batiste etc., used for the making of undergarments.

Lingerie set (*Parure*) - matching feminine undergarments.

Mamillare - See Strophium

Monokini (See also Swimsuit) - Swimsuit that appeared in the 60s which originally consisted of trunks held up by braces which left the breasts partially naked. It will later transform to the topless, consisting of the bottom half of a two-piece swimsuit.

Negligee - (See also Dressing Gown) A garment made of very light, flimsy fabric that women wore at home and, in some cases, to receive close friends at the end of the 19th century.

Nightdress - Nightdresses were worn very sporadically by both men and women over the centuries. From the 11th to the 16th centuries, nudity at night was standard practice. But from the 15th century, new mothers being visited by friends started to wear nightdresses. The shape of nightdresses was similar to that of undershirts. In the 18th century, nightdresses became longer for women but there was no change for men until pyjamas appeared. In the 19th century the proliferation of undergarments which concealed the body, made them more erotic. Consequently nightdresses started to be embellished with embroideries and lace insertions. In the 20s night dresses alternate with pyjamas. In 1930 nightdresses were made of embroidered satin with lace insertions, skirts were cut on the bias and backs were very low so that they were very similar in design to fashionable evening dresses. In the 40s nylon was in vogue and was often used for nightdresses because it did not crease and was very transparent.

Nightie - See Baby-doll and Nightdress.

Pannier (See also Crinoline) - Boned underskirt used for widening women's skirts. Panniers appeared after the "criardes", petticoats made of gummed rustling fabric. When the pannier appeared in 1718, it was round and bell-shaped, between 1725 and 1730 it became oval, in 1730 it became flat in the front, then in 1750 it split into two. Panniers, the shape of which could vary so much, were used until the Revolution.

Panties - Until the 30s, panties (pants) were shaped like a petticoat with legs. In accordance with the "infantilization" trend that influenced clothing in general, women imitated children as they adopted short and close-fitting panties inspired from the famous panties made by *Petit Bateau*. Panties will later on become smaller and transform into their even tinier version, bikini panties (called *slip* in French from the English "to slip") which were very narrow on the hips.

Petticoat - The word "petticoat" appeared in the 16th century along with the word "skirt" designating a garment worn by women extending from the waist down to the feet. From the 16th to the 18th centuries, petticoat meant a short under-skirt worn under other skirts and, at the end of the 18th and 19th centuries, it described the skirt over which the dress opened. It was only in 1890 that the word petticoat came to mean an undergarment.

Pouf - See Bustle

Pyjamas - The name originated from the Hindustani, *apae-jama*, the word for women's trousers. This night-time garment was worn by both men and women from the 20s. For women pyjamas were more sophisticated and feminine (in shape, prints and colours). In those days, pyjamas were also worn at the seaside as a swimming costume or at home where they were seen as more convenient and comfortable than the negligee.

Stockings - These derived from knee breeches which were close-fitting garments for men covering legs from the foot up to the knee. Ordinary stockings were made of wool whereas luxury stockings were in silk (from 1527 when knitting machines appeared in England). Cotton stockings were popular during the last third of the 18th century and lisle thread was very fashionable in the reign of Louis Philippe. At the end of the 19th century, silk was used for stockings and for other undergarments. After 1924 as skirts got shorter, flesh-coloured silk stockings became more popular. Late in the 20s, hosiers started to use rayon — also called synthetic silk. It was 1938 that nylon stockings appeared, together with nylon itself which was developed by the Du Pont de Nemours Company. Because of the restrictions imposed during World War II, women adopted an amazing subterfuge: they dyed their legs then painted, behind the calf, a brown line imitating the stocking seam. In 1955 seamed stockings disappeared, thanks to a new weaving technique. In the 60s the stocking industry underwent radical changes with the creation of tights that will considerably improve in the 70s (the mesh becomes finer). As attractive undergarments were again in fashion in the 80s, stockings were

restored to favour and tights became more sophisticated. Back seams were incorporated, and new textures used — fine mesh lace, printed nylon, embroidered fabrics, or designs studded with paste "gem" stones. Some were made partly of silk.

Strophium - This was the ancestor of the bra, and was a rolled scarf wound round the body many times to support the breasts. It was put in place on top of a little tunic, whereas the *mamillare*, another accessory used to support the breasts, was worn right next to the skin.

Suspender belt (See also Suspenders) - A narrow belt with suspenders attached to support women's stockings — suspender belts appeared around 1910, as corsets and all their accessories were becoming less and less popular.

Suspenders - Rubber straps attached to the corset, girdle or garter belt, with fastenings to hold up stockings. Around 1862 the straps were slipped through buckles attached to the stockings themselves, but that system disappeared in 1900 mainly because of the adoption at the same time of the long, straight-fronted corset. Suspenders then had the advantage of keeping up the stockings and pulling the corset forward, so that the busk would not press too hard on the stomach and the corset would fall straight. Suspenders will be used until elastic girdles appeared and then also to prevent the girdles from rolling up on the hips.

Swimsuit - In 1880, women's swimsuits consisted of an ample tunic caught in at the waist plus long underpants that covered the legs down to the ankles. It is only around 1925 that the one-piece close-fitting swimsuit revealing the legs and arms appeared. The two-piece swimsuit with separate top and bottom will appear around 1935 and it's in 1946 that the bikini will become popular. The popularity of the monokini with straps in the 60s and later of the topless look (in vogue nowadays) proves that swimsuits have a tendency to disappear leading to a complete nudity that is fully accepted.

Tea-gown - Negligee shaped like a dressing gown worn at tea time to entertain friends.

Tights - (See also Stockings) Fine-meshed, close-fitting (thus the name) tights appeared in 1958 and covered the body from the waist, where it was tightened by elastic, down to the feet. It was still too early and tights were only adopted in 1960 when the mini-skirt appeared.

Undershirt - See Chemise

Whalebone - Flexible strips of bone, horn, metal or plastic used to reinforce various parts of the corset. For some time corset makers used real whalebones, which could be two metres long and which grow in place of teeth in the upper jaw of whales.

Whalebone bodice - In the 16th century, with the influence of Spanish fashion, women used to wear a kind of camisole stiffened by a busk meant to shape and control the bust and the waist. In the 17th and 18th centuries, the body was enclosed in a tight-fitting laced, boned corselet. In will disappear late in the 18th century and will be replaced by the corset (a looser bodice with fewer bones) which will itself disappear with the introduction of neo-classical fashion.

Waspie - A type of corset designed to make the waist slender. It was created in 1945 by Marcel Rochas. It heralded the return to close-fitting garments confirmed in 1947 by Dior with his "New Look".

Zona - An undergarment that appeared in Greece in the 9th century B.C. It was a flat wide belt wound around the waist at the hips and worn only by maidens. They discarded this belt during the marriage ceremony when it was untied by the husband. It was not a supporting accessory but rather a symbolic garment.

BIBLIOGRAPHY

I - General studies
BOUCHER François, *Histoire du costume en Occident de l'Antiquité à nos jours*, Paris, Flammarion, 1965-1983.

BUTAZZI Grazietta, *La mode, art, histoire et société*, Milan, G.E. Fabbri, 1981 - Paris, Hachette, 1983.

CHALLAMEL Augustin, *Histoire de la mode en France, la toilette des femmes depuis l'époque gallo-romaine*, Paris, A. Hennuyer imp., 1881, in-8°.

DAVENPORT Millia, *The book of costume*, New York, Crown publishers, 2 volumes, in-4°.

HAUSEN Henny Harald, *Histoire du costume*, translated from the Danish by Jacqueline Puissant, Paris, Flammarion, 1956, in-8°.

LAVER James, *The literature of fashion*, Cambridge University Press, London, the Shenval Press, 1947, in-8°.

LAVER James, *Taste and fashion from the French Revolution to the present day*, London, G.G. Harrap, 1948, in-8°.

LELOIR Maurice, *Dictionnaire du costume et de ses accessoires, des armes et des étoffes des origines à nos jours*, completed under the direction of André Dupuis, Paris, Gründ (Vanves), 1951, in-8°.

LELOIR Maurice, *Histoire du costume de l'Antiquité à 1914*, Paris, Henri Ernest, 1934.

QUICHERAT Jules, *Histoire du costume en France depuis les temps les plus reculés jusqu'à la fin du XVIII° s.*, Paris, Hachette, 1875, in-8°.

RACINET Auguste, *Le costume historique*, Paris, Fiermin-Didot, 1888, in 6 volumes.

II - Specific Studies

a/ Greece and Rome
HEUZEY Jacques, *Histoire du costume antique*, Honoré Champion bookshop, 1922.

HEUZEY Jacques, *Le costume féminin en Grèce à l'époque archaïque*, in-4°, extract from "Gazette des beaux-arts", April 1938.

RICH Anthony, *Dictionnaire des antiquités romaines et grecques*, Paris, Firmin-Didot, 1859, in-8°.

b/ Egypt and Mesopotamia
BONNET Hans, *Die A Egyptishe Tracht bis zum Ende des neuen Reiches*, Leipzig, Hinrichs'sche Buchlandlung, 1917, in-4°.

GAYET A., *Le costume en Egypte du III° au XV° siècles*, Paris, Ernest Leroux, 1900, in-12°.

HOUSTON Mary G., *Ancient Egyptian Mesopotamian and Persian costume and decoration*, London, Adam and Charles, 1954, in-8°.

c/ The Middle Ages
ENLART Camille, *Manuel d'archéologie française depuis les temps mérovingiens jusqu'à la Renaissance*, book III, *Le costume*, Paris, Auguste Picard, 1916, in-8°.

PEIGNOT Gabriel, *Choix de testaments anciens et modernes*, Paris, Renouard, 1829, in 8°.

d/ From the 17th century
BOUCHOT Henri, *Le luxe française, I. L'Empire*, Paris, Librairie illustrée, 1882, in-8°. *II La Restauration*, 1893, in-8°.

BOUCHOT Henri, *Les élégances du Second Empire*, Paris, Librairie illustrée 1896, in-16°.

LAMESANGERE Pierre de, *Observations sur les modes et les usages de Paris pour servir d'explication aux caricatures publiées sous le titre de « Bon Genre » depuis le commencement du XIX° siècle*, Paris, bd Montmartre n° 1, 1827, in-fol.

MERCIER Louis-Sébastien, *Tableau de Paris*, Amsterdam, 1783.

MERCIER Louis-Sébastien, *Le nouveau Paris*, 1862, Poulet-Malassis, in-18°.

e/ And in particular
DUFAY Pierre, *Le pantalon féminin*, Paris, Charles Carrington ed., 1906, in-12°.

EWING Elisabeth, *Dress and undress, A history of women's underwear*, Drama Book specialists, New York, 1978.

FASHION INSTITUTE OF TECHNOLOGY (F.I.T.), *The undercover story*, exhibition catalogue F.I.T., New York, 1985.

FLOBERT Laure, *La femme et le costume masculin*, Lille, Lefebvre-Ducrocq printery, 1911.

GRAND-CARTERET John, *La femme en culotte*, Paris Flammarion, in-12°.

LA FIZELIERE Albert de, *Histoire de la crinoline au temps passé, suivie de la satire sur les cerceaux, paniers, etc., par le Chevalier de Wisard*, Paris, A. Aubry, 1859, in-18°.

LEOTY Ernest, *Le corset à travers les âges*, Paris, Paul Ollendorff, 1893, in-4°.

LIBRON F. and CLOUZOT H., *Le corset dans l'art et les mœurs du XIII° au XIX°*, Paris, Libron, 1932.

PEARCE Arthur W., *The Future out of the Past*, illustrated history of Warner Brothers, USA, published by Warner, 1964.

WAUGH Norah, *Corsets and crinolines*, B.T., Batsford Ltd, London, 1954.

PHOTO CREDITS

◆

pp. 2 and 3: Rapho.
p. 10: Rapho.
p. 11: Sunset Boulevard.
p. 14: rights reserved.
p. 15: rights reserved.
p. 16: John Kacere, OK Harris (USA), Jean-Pierre Lavigne gallery (France).
p. 17: Lauros-Giraudon, Paris, coll. part., A.D.A.G.P.
p. 22: Rapho, Délos Museum.
p. 23: *La peinture grecque*, by Martin Robertson (c) 1959 by Ed. d'Art A. Skira, Geneva.
p. 24: *La peinture égyptienne*, by Arpag Mekhitarian (c) 1954 by Ed. d'Art A. Skira, Geneva.
p. 25: top, Cicione-Rapho; below *La peinture égyptienne*, by Arpag Mekhitarian (c) 1954 by Ed. d'Art A. Skira, Geneva.
p. 26: Giraudon.
p. 27: Leonard Von Matt-Rapho.
p. 28: top, Bulloz, Paris, musée du Petit Palais; below, Rapho, Delphi Museum.
p. 29: Giraudon.
p. 30: top, Giraudon; below, Louis Frederic-Rapho.
p. 31: *La peinture grecque* by Martin Robertson (c) 1959 by Ed. d'Art A. Skira, Geneva.
p. 32: top, Bulloz, Rome, below Giraudon, Paris, Louvre.
p. 33: Giraudon, Paris, Louvre.
p. 34: Giraudon, Naples, national archeological museum.
p. 35: Giraudon, Pompéi, house of mysteries.
p. 36: Georges Viollon-Rapho.
p. 37: Georges Viollon-Rapho.
p. 38: vignette, Bulloz, Naples Museum; right, Bulloz, Paris, Louvre.
p. 39: Bulloz, Paris, Louvre.
p. 40: Kay Lawson-Rapho.
p. 41: Giraudon, Naples, National Museum.
p. 42: Scala-Firenze.
p. 44: Giraudon, Poitiers, bibl. municipale.
p. 45: Giraudon, Toulouse musée des Augustins.
p. 46: Giraudon, Paris, Louvre.
p. 47: Giraudon.
p. 48: Giraudon, Strasbourg, musée de lœuvre N.D.
p. 49: Lauros-Giraudon, Laon, bibl. municipale.
p. 50: BN.
p. 51: Giraudon, Paris, BN.
p. 52: Giraudon, Paris, BN.
P. 53: top, Giraudon, Nantes; below Giraudon.
p. 54: top, Bulloz, Paris, BN; below, Lauros-Giraudon, Chantilly, musée de Condé.
p. 55: top, BN; below, Lauros-Giraudon, Chantilly, musée de Condé.
p. 57: Giraudon, Paris, bibl. de l'Arsenal.
p. 58: top, Bulloz, Paris, Petit Palais; below, Giraudon, Paris, bibl. de l'Arsenal.
p. 59: top at right, Giraudon, Paris, archives nationales; left, below, Giraudon, Chantilly, musée de Condé.
p. 60: Bulloz, Paris, Louvre.
p. 62: Giraudon, Montpellier, Hôtel de Lunaret.
p. 63 top, Giraudon, Rennes, musée des Bx Arts; below, gruppo editoriale Fabbri, Bompiani, Sonzogno, Etas. S.p.a. Milan, Poldi Pezzoli Museum.
p. 64: right, Giraudon, Dijon, musée des Bx Arts.
p. 66: top, Victoria and Albert museum; below F.I.T., exhibition catalogue, *The undercover story*, photo: Seth Joel.
p. 67: Giraudon, Valenciennes, musée des Bx Arts.
p. 68: Bulloz, St-Omer.
p. 70: Giraudon, Chartres, musée des Bx Arts.
p. 72: centre, Victoria and Albert museum.
p. 75: left, Bulloz, musée Carnavalet.
p. 76: Bulloz, musée Carnavalet.
p. 77: Roger Viollet, BN.
p. 78: top, Roger Viollet, musée Carnavalet; below Giraudon.
p. 79: top, Bulloz, musée Cognacq-Jay; below, Bulloz, priv. coll.
p. 80: top, Giraudon, Marseille.
p. 81: top, Bulloz, musée Carnavalet.
p. 86: top, Giraudon, Paris, BN; below, Roger Viollet.
p. 87: Roger Viollet.
p. 88: top, Roger Viollet.
p. 90: BBC Hulton Picture Library.
p. 91: top, Roger Viollet.
p. 92: top, Roger Viollet; below Photo-Publi-Presse.
p. 93: top, Royal Photographic Society; below, Roger Viollet.
p. 94: below, Roger Viollet.
p. 95: top, Photo-Publi-Presse.
p. 96: top, BN; below, Roger Viollet.
p. 97: Bulloz.
p. 98: top, BBC Hulton Picture Library; below, at left, Roger Viollet, Bibl. de l'Opéra de Paris; right, Roger Viollet.
p. 99: centre, Roger Viollet; right, BBC Hulton Picture Library.
p. 100: F.I.T., New York.
p. 101: below, Boubat-agence Top.
p. 102: BBC Hulton Picture Library.
p. 103: Roger Viollet.
p. 104: Roger Viollet.
p. 105: top, BBC Hulton Picture Library; below, Roger Viollet.
p. 107: BN.
p. 109: Lauros-Giraudon, Paris, musée Carnavalet.
p. 110: Roger Viollet, BN.
pp. 112, 113, 114, 115: BBC Hulton Picture Library.
p. 116: Roger Viollet.
p. 118: Henriette Angel.
p. 119: top, Lauros-Giraudon, Paris, musée Carnavalet.
pp. 120-121: Brooklyn museum.
p. 122: below left, Roger Viollet; centre, Henriette Angel.
p. 123: top, Henriette Angel; below, BBC Hulton Picture Library.
p. 124: Brooklyn museum.
p. 125: photo Chantal Fribourg, extract from exhibition catalogue of *Secrets d'Elégance* 1750/1950, musée de la mode et du costume.
p. 128: F.I.T., exhibition catalogue, *The undercover story*, photo Seth Joel.
p. 129: F.I.T., New York.
p. 130: F.I.T., exhibition catalogue, *The undercover story*, photo Seth Joel.
p. 131: F.I.T., New York.
p. 132: The museum of Modern Art, New York; The Abbot-Levy collection, partial gift of Shirley C. Burden.
p. 133: top, Leicestershire museums, Symington collection.
p. 139: Brooklyn museum, gift of E.A. Meister.
p. 141: Henriette Angel.
p. 142: photos Chantal Fribourg, extract from exhibition catalogue of *Secrets d'Elégance* 1750/1950, musée de la mode et du costume.
p. 143: Roger Viollet.
p. 144: Bulloz, Douai, Spadem.
p. 145: below, Photo-Publi-Presse.
p. 146: BBC Hulton Picture Library.
p. 147: top, Bulloz, muzée de Sceaux, Spadem; below, BBC Hulton Picture Library.
p. 153: photo Chantal Fribourg, extract from exhibition catalogue of *Secrets d'Elégance* 1750/1950, musée de la mode et du costume.
p. 159: association des amis de Jacques-Henri Lartigue - Spadem.
p. 160: Bulloz, musée de Nancy, Spadem.
p. 161: top, Henriette Angel.
p. 162: Roger Viollet.
p. 165: Leicestershire museums, the Symington collection.
p. 166: below left, BN; centre, BBC Hulton Picture Library.
p. 167: BBC Hulton Picture Library.
p. 169: Roger Viollet.
p. 178: Roger Viollet.
p. 187: BBC Hulton Picture Library.
p. 189: below, BBC Hulton Picture Library.
p. 190: F.I.T. New York.
p. 191: top and below, at left, F.I.T., New York.
p. 194: U.F.A.C., Vogue, rights reserved.
pp. 196–197: top, left and centre, F.I.T. New York.
p. 198: top, Horst, rights reserved; below, Robert Capa-Magnum.
p. 199: (c) Vere French.
p. 201: Rapho.
p. 202: BBC Hulton Picture Library.
p. 203: below, BBC Hulton Picture Library.
p. 204: Schirmer/Mosel München, 1984.
p. 205: Bartsch and Chariau Gallery, Munich.
p. 210: U.F.A.C., don de Claude Salvy, rights reserved.
p. 211: centre, Leonard Freed-Magnum.
pp. 212-213: Paul de Cordon/Crazy Horse.
pp. 214-215: Sunset Boulevard.
p. 219: left, Seeberger, BN; right, Photo-Publi-Presse.
pp. 220-221: Marie-Claire.
pp. 224-225: U.F.A.C. rights reserved.
p. 226: Helmut Newton-Vogue Germany.
p. 227: U.F.A.C. rights reserved.
p. 228: left, U.F.A.C., rights reserved; right, Marie-Claire.
p. 229: U.F.A.C., rights reserved
p. 230: U.F.A.C., rights reserved
p. 231: left, Rapho; right, U.F.A.C., rights reserved.
p. 232: Elle.
p. 233: U.F.A.C., rights reserved.
p. 236: U.F.A.C., rights reserved.
p. 237: Photo-Publi-Presse.
p. 238: John Kacere - OK Harris (USA)/Jean-Pierre Lavigne Gallery (France).
p. 239: Elle.
p. 241: Mannequin: Janice Dickinson.
p. 242: Helmut Newton-Vogue France.
p. 243: Magnum.
p. 246: Marie-Claire.
p. 247: l'Etichetta.
p. 249: Figaro Madame.
p. 252: Figaro Madame.
p. 253: Elle.
pp. 258-259: Marie-Claire.
p. 260: top, Cent idées; below Elle.
p. 261: Marie-Claire.
pp. 264-265: Dépêche Mode SA, mannequin: Micheline Van de Velde.

We would like to thank:
— all the manufacturers cited in this book and in particular those who helped us to gather the necessary information and documentation: Antinéa, Aubade (Annie Bredin), Chantal Thomass, Cadolle, Dim, Dior (Mr Bardin and Mr Bob de Tournemire), Gemma (Guy Bruny), Gossard, La Perla (Mr Borgomanero), Rigby and Peller, Rosy, Sabbia Rosa, Warner (Mr Bodard and Mr Cadoux);
— the French Federation of Corset Manufacturers represented by Miss Morizet who kindly provided us with their archives;
— Mrs Evans who was our valuable contact in Great Britain;
— Mr Jose Alvarez;
— photographers' agents, Suzanne Dalton, Barbara Schlager and, in particular, Kaze Kuramochi whose suggestions have been invaluable.
— the OK Harris Gallery (U.S.A.) and the Jean-Pierre Lavigne Gallery (France);
— all the photographers who kindly contributed to this book, Jean François Bauret, François-Xavier Bouchart, Arthur Elgort, Franco, F. Giacobetti, Fujiii Hideki, Steve Hiett, Lionel Kazan, Eddy Kohli, Inakoshi Koichi, Paul Lange, J.F. Lepage, Peter Linberg, Miseki Liu Simon, Sarah Moon, Christian Moser, Catherine Panchout, Marc Picot, François Pomepui, Bettina Rheims, Tony Thorimbert, Oliviero Toscani, Ukiyoe Kuzushi, Clauss Wickrath, Mike Yavel, and, in particular, Helmut Newton and Jeanloup Sieff.
Finally we would like to thank the models who posed for this book and whose names we unfortunately cannot list.

PRINTED IN SINGAPORE
AUGUST, 1986

280